THE ANGLICAN CHURCH
TODAY AND TOMORROW

THE ANGLICAN CHURCH TODAY AND TOMORROW

by

Michael Marshall

Director of the Anglican Institute, St Louis, USA
former Bishop of Woolwich (1975–84)

Morehouse Barlow
Wilton

Dedicated to
Eric Abbott
(1906–83)
priest and friend

'He loved the Church of England'

Copyright © Michael Marshall 1984

First published 1984
by A. R. Mowbray & Co. Ltd.
Saint Thomas House, Becket Street
Oxford, OX1 1SJ

ISBN 0 264 66940 1

First American edition published 1984
by Morehouse Barlow Co., Inc.
78 Danbury Road
Wilton, Connecticut 06897

ISBN 0 8192 1341 1

British Library Cataloguing in Publication Data

Marshall, Michael, 1936-
    The Anglican Church today and tomorrow.—
    (Christian studies series)
    1. Anglican Communion
    I. Title II. Series
    283   BX5005

ISBN 0-264-66940-1

Library of Congress Catalog Card Number 83-62718
Printed in the United States of America

Author's Note

Conception is one thing: birth is a much longer and more hazardous process and frequently requires help from a whole team of patient friends and supporters. So it is with a book.

Canon William Purcell has been a most patient and encouraging help – not least because this particular 'baby' was long overdue! Without Mary Baddeley, my secretary, who has always typed all my manuscripts and previous books over many years, I would never have completed this (or indeed any other) literary task. I also wish to record my gratitude to Charles Bewick who tackled the exacting task of notes and references, as well as to Paul Jobson who gave considerable help in the practicalities of producing several copies of several revisions of several manuscripts! I should also like to thank Rosemary Bourne of Mowbrays Publishing Division for going beyond the call of duty in her careful work on proofs.

M.M.

Contents

Preface

I would never have chosen to write this book! Perhaps that is the best sort of book to write – the book you were invited to write. However, in retrospect, I am most grateful to have had the opportunity to read and re-read many of the classics of Anglicanism and to have been compelled to sit down and consider my Anglican calling.

For, in fact I am Anglican by conviction and not by convenience. Since I have been writing this book, at various conferences and in groups where I have been present I have frequently asked for a show of hands, first from those who were baptized as Anglicans and then from those who became Anglicans by choice from one or other of the Christian denominations. Almost always, the last group has been in the majority. Surely that tells us something about the very nature of the Anglican Church.

Certainly in my own case, my decision to become an Anglican after a strong Roman Catholic upbringing, was far from an easy choice. Over the years, the strains and tensions within Anglicanism (not least since I have been a bishop) have tempted me at times to seek the shelter of a more secure and apparently more consistent Church. Yet, in my heart of hearts, the pages of this book are for me a living testimony to the strengths and weaknesses of a gospel Church, which demands the strenuous exercise of mind and conscience and which refuses to be over-protective against the winds and storms of unbelief and the challenges which inevitably come to us from the world in which we live. Bishop Gerald Ellison wrote: 'To be an Anglican requires many qualities which even some men of highest religious genius have lacked. It requires the courage to apply the individual conscience to the challenge of the Faith; it needs the patience to wait till the answer to some problem not yet obvious is revealed, and the honesty on occasions to say, "I don't know". It needs the love to be tolerant with those whom we think misguided or foolish in the expression of their opinions. It needs the self-discipline to accept the demands of our faith, not because we are told we must do so, but because we believe such things to be true. Here is the true genius of Anglicanism; and it is very precious.'[1]

Yes, it is very precious and yet it is also very painful. However, do not let it be thought that this book is an attempt to reassert denominationalism. The author is far too aware of the failings and pitfalls of Anglicanism at the present time, as well as being someone who is far too committed to Christian unity, to allow such a retrograde step to be taken in his name.

No, first and foremost it is addressed to Anglicans at a time when we need to put our own house in order. We need to be recalled to our theological mandate and to avoid party divisions and fragmentation. If what is written in these pages is the theological mandate of Anglicanism, it will both place certain restraints upon us as well as open up for us particular responsibilities and rich opportunities, not least in respect of our responsibilities to our fellow Christians in other Churches. Furthermore, it is addressed primarily to the serious enquirer (and not to theologians) as a guide-book to Anglican theology and as a rationale for Anglican witness. It is hoped therefore that it will speak in the present climate to a vast resurgence of religious interest, not least among young people, which has so far been largely unrelated to the life of the mainstream Churches. It is a time for do-it-yourself religion, in pursuit of kicks and new experiences, with everything from alternative medicine to the occult, astrology, TM and drugs. Gerald Priestland rightly comments: 'Do-it-yourself religion can go crazy: there's no nut like a religious nut!'[2] He is right, and yet the Churches have a real responsibility to meet this new interest in religion and rescue it from some of the worst pitfalls of fundamentalism and from the manipulation and tyranny which are already evident in the lives of the disciples of many new sects and fringe churches today, not only in America, but also in the UK and many parts of the world.

It is against this background of the call to unity and also at the same time to mission, evangelism and renewal that this book is written. Both of these goals are best pursued in relation to each other and not in isolation from each other. The tendency to isolate them has persisted for far too long. Anglicanism has, I believe, particular credentials which demand that it should seek to serve aims which are wider than its own survival. In the end, that is most likely to help us to put our own house in order, for it should rescue the whole exercise from being simply a piece of domestic reordering and spring-cleaning (for this book is not an attempt to make Anglicans house-proud). It should help us to throw open the doors and windows of *ecclesia anglicana*, both in order to let in air and light (both of them significant ingredients, present at the first Pentecost) and then to expel us into a world where we shall lose our self-consciousness and be caught up in a vision which is ready to go to nothing less than the ends of the earth (again the distinctive dynamic of the first Pentecost).

6 August 1983   † Michael Woolwich
Feast of the Transfiguration

NOTES

1. G. Ellison, *The Anglican Communion*, Seabury Press, New York, 1960, p. 84
2. Gerald Priestland, *Thought for the Day*, BBC, 6 July 1983

1. The contemporary religious supermarket

1. Signs of religious revival today

All the signs would seem to suggest that, certainly in the closing decades of the twentieth century and possibly in the opening decades of the twenty-first century (should it ever dawn), there will be a period of renewed resurgence in religious interest throughout the world. Such a statement may not in fact come as quite such a surprise today as it would have done in the fifties and sixties of this century. Certainly in the western world, after the war, and in areas where Christianity was the dominant religion, while 'God talk' in any shape or form seemed to be very piano indeed, at the same time atheistic philosophies were apparently entering a recurring passage in their history, conspicuously marked 'crescendo'. Of course, it is all too easy, with hindsight, to claim that for those with 'ears to hear' and 'eyes to see' (and indeed with any sense of history or understanding of human nature at all), an era of militant materialism and confident humanism can generally be guaranteed soon to make way for a subsequent chapter of confident (if somewhat undiscriminating) religious revival. The psychologist Jung, in many of his writings, had confidently foretold such an era of religious revival. Largely he regarded it as springing from a disenchantment with materialism. He writes: 'The rapid and world-wide growth of a psychological interest over the last two decades shows unmistakably that modern man has to some extent turned his attention from material things to his own subjective processes.'[1]

In any case, it is clear to see that once you put the cat of religious experience out of the back door of human life, it will not be long before the tiger of religious revival and enthusiasm will come pounding up the front path demanding a dramatic, popular (and frequently unquestioned) return through the front door of human history. For men and women are religi-

1

ous animals, and sooner or later they demand a specifically religious ingredient in their daily diet. So perhaps we should not be quite so surprised to find that, after a chapter of confident materialism, especially after the Second World War (at least in the western affluent world), religion in many and varying shapes and sizes is back again. Indeed, Alvin Toffler, in his remarkably prophetic book, *The Third Wave*, is prepared to go as far as speaking of 'waves of religious revivalism' *crashing* through 'Libya, Syria, the United States of America'[2] and many parts of the world as the twentieth century draws to a close.

It is not the purpose of this book to examine in any detail the many reasons which determine the persistence of religion at every turn in the story of mankind. Suffice it to say, that evidence from many disciplines and sciences is overwhelmingly unanimous in endorsing the importance and place of the religious instinct which is never far beneath the surface in human history. In other words, throughout every language and culture the word 'god' always holds some place in the human vocabulary. Neither obsession with material things on the one hand, nor political oppression and atheistic totalitarian regimes on the other hand, have ever succeeded in removing the name of the deity from human lips, nor a thirst and desire for the sacred from human hearts. From Nero to Stalin and from Hitler's attempted extinction of the Jews to the Marxist murder of millions of Christians in our own day, the pattern of suppression and revival has always been the same. Materialistic obsession is the most obvious prelude to spiritual curiosity, and the blood of martyrs has consistently been the perennial seed of sturdy and resilient faith. Of course, as we shall see (and this is very much the purpose of this book), men have meant very different things by the one word 'religion'; and it must be frankly and freely admitted that the little word 'god' in every language has been used and abused as the excuse for every atrocity under the sun. Not all religions are good. Some are better than others and indeed we have to admit that, if in the end there is only one God, then not all conflicting religious claims can be equally valid in the truth which they seek to proclaim. What is quite certain is that religion is far from harmless, that religious wars are always the bloodiest, and that when religion goes wrong it goes really wrong and is not just harmless or a little bit mistaken. In other words, the religious instinct which is in mankind is never neutral and frequently dangerous. It is especially dangerous when it is allowed to go unchecked by other instincts, or when it is encouraged to sweep all before it in 'waves of religious revivalism'.

2. Faith or fear?

For, although it must be freely admitted that the basis of all true religion must be faith, yet it is often fear (the very opposite of faith) which drives men and women to seek a ready-made faith which will meet their needs and protect them from the storms and fortunes of life and history. Little wonder, then, that periods of stability, prosperity and complacency have frequently been chapters of low religious motivation, either in the history of a nation or culture or in our personal lives, while other times of instability, hardship and suffering, with all their attendant fears, often lead to a zealous religious quest. Although it should not be so, we have to admit that God is seldom on the lips of the prosperous and the complacent (except perhaps as a word of blasphemy) while on the other hand, drowning men (if subsequently recovered) will freely and eloquently admit, without apology, their cry for help to the Almighty as vivid, unforgettable and uppermost in their experience of panic, fear and desperation.

We could well ask, therefore, whether the principle motivation at work in the contemporary religious revival in our world – not only in Christianity but also in other major world religions – is not mainly based on fear. Certainly it would not be surprising if the present climate of instability and apprehension around the whole subconscious fear of a nuclear holocaust gave way to a strong sense, throughout the whole world, of living on a precipice. At such times, the cynic will frequently remind us, men turn to religion in the hope of finding solace, meaning, purpose and an inner stability – the opium of the masses. Hopefully, this fear will not be the only ingredient which motivates a return to religious faith; but, if the religion which is sought is largely seen as 'an answer' to fear, disintegration and instability, the chances are that it will be a distorted religion, powerful in its claims, even possibly impressive in its achievements, yet disastrous in its side effects and ultimately leading its new disciples further away from true freedom, maturity and fullness of life.

Few would doubt, at least in America at the present time, that the manipulation of sects in the Christian religion is an alarming phenomenon. Many of these sects – counted currently at over two hundred and fifty – are extreme evangelical sectarian churches, under the leadership of a charismatic character whose ministry is very close to a personality cult. Alvin Toffler writes: 'More important than the growing human-potential industry is the Christian evangelical movement. Appealing to poorer and less educated segments of the public, making sophisticated use of high-powered radio and television, the "born-again" movement is ballooning in size. Religious hucksters, riding its crest, send their followers scrambling for salvation in a society they picture as decadent and doomed'.[3] Much of the impetus for these 'ballooning' churches stems, Toffler believes, from despair and fear in an age of apparent disintegration and instability. 'We see,' he writes, 'a wildfire revival of fundamentalist religion and a desperate search for something – almost anything – to believe in.'[4] He sees the decay of the industrial society in the west as responsible for leaving 'millions of people grasping desperately for something to hold on to – anything, from Texas Taoism to Swedish Sufism, from Philippine faith-healing to Welsh witchcraft'.[5] He speaks alarmingly of a 'spiritual supermarket, with its depressing razzmatazz and religious fakery'[6] dangerously lurking with 'cult-based political movements headed by ayatollahs named Smith, Schultz or Santini', running for power in politics on the crude 'law-and-order' or 'anti-porn' programmes with a strong authoritarian streak: all as yet perhaps only a 'glimmering intimation of the religio-politics that may well lie ahead even in the most secular of societies'.[7]

4

Neither must we suppose that this is only, or largely, an American disease: we have more than our fair share of such extreme sects in England. It is true that they are often popularized in a different key and in more sober tones, advertising as philosophical societies, schools or meditation groups; but the end result is often the same or very similar to the more abrasive and hysterical forms of religious revivalism in the United States. Lives are dominated; rules are enforced; powerful promises and claims are made, and in the end (and this is the note of pastoral urgency) disciples are duped and lives are seriously maimed, if not destroyed.

Although we may not feel the need to endorse all the implications of Toffler's thesis, there is enough overlap between what he has written and predicted and what is already happening in the great religious scene of the western world (at least) to give cause for alarm and to demand from Christian and other religious leaders a sober diagnosis linked to some kind of corrective programme. The events of the People's Temple in Guyana in 1979 should not be seen as typical, and yet it is not so wholly untypical as to be written off as an isolated and unrepresentative aberration. It had about it many characteristics which are common to many contemporary religions and Christian sects today. Each characteristic has always had its part to play in religious experience, but in isolation and unchecked, it steers its disciples into the realms of fanaticism and into the bondage of zealous extremism.

Perhaps the most striking and pervasive feature in the present climate of religious revivalism, is that recurring theme in periods of instability and violent change throughout history: the millennium instinct – that impending sense of the end of all things. Such an 'instinct' is stimulated from many quarters today, many of them rooted more in the secular sensitivities of the younger generation than in the specifically religious realm. Fear of a nuclear catastrophe is once again very much in the forefront of people's minds throughout the whole world. In a recent questionnaire, over seventy per cent of people under the age of twenty-one expected that the world would not reach the end of the present century without a major nuclear disaster on a world-wide scale. Popular fiction, from the pens of authors such as Morris West, speak almost prophetically of the end of society as we presently know it. Impending doom, decay and disaster is the theme of many recent films, novels, plays and pop songs, all pervading our collective subconscious with a deep sense of 'fear and with foreboding of what is coming on the world'.[8]

Such a climate is, and always has been, throughout history, a breeding ground for extreme sectarian groups, who take the theme of the millennium as the whole basis for their spirituality. They literally flee to the 'mountain tops' or out into 'the desert places', sharing some kind of common life, simple diet and a long agenda of stern austerities, where they purport to wait and prepare for the end of all things. Their message gains power and immediacy from the unquestioned millennium mystique which forms the ground base of all the other themes to which they seek to witness and to which their discipleship is directed.

Strongly linked to this outlook, is the following of messianic figures which pop out of the woodwork of history at times like this. Using the vast market of the media (especially in America), charismatic figures emerge and rapidly manipulate a huge industry of evangelism and indoctrination. They sell their wares because they are able to give to people what people appear to need: a dose of religion which makes them feel better. For too long, the established mainstream Churches have ignored the emotions and feelings and have (rightly) pointed to the dangers of purely subjective feelings as the reliable barometer of spiritual growth. So, on the one hand, while the more mainstream Churches have been pointing away from emotions and the cult of religious experiences, at the same time, others have reached into the vacuum of religious experiences, so evident in our western world, and filled it with substitutes of many kinds, all of which seem to have one thing in common: pragmatism and the ever increasing chorus of popular religious affirmation expressed in the naive words: 'But it really does work!'

Ever since Descartes (1596–1650), not only in the secular

6

world of education, but also in the religious communication of varying 'gospels', there has been an over-emphasis laid upon the place of the mind and the reason in assessing religion and all other truths. In order to validate anything and everything it must be rationally defensible. While this has been the programme at one level, at the same time, at another level (more subtle and more sinister) neglected emotions and disturbed emotions, which have been left unexercised and remain unchecked or unexplored, will acquire a new power and a dangerous and distinctive thrust. The rationalist of one age is nearly always the father of the mindless enthusiast of the next generation. Little wonder, therefore, that much of the present religious revivalism draws new energies from the neglected forces of emotionalism so strongly repressed by earlier generations. It is almost as though there were two currents passing each other in the night in the sixties and seventies of the present century. On the one hand, the established mainstream Churches were reducing necessary beliefs to a minimum and editing out everything of the cult, of mystery and anything which demanded belief rather than mere understanding. Passing in the other direction, and at the same time, was an upsurge of mindless religious enthusiasm seeking evermore the place of the cult and the mysterious and always ready to believe anything and everything, providing it worked and providing it brought with it therapeutic support and solace.

Furthermore, the sheer aridity of much religious education and communication in recent decades was never likely to equip disciples with the necessary intellectual and rational knowledge necessary to combat fundamentalism in its many shapes and sizes. In the case of the Christian gospel a little knowledge certainly proved to be a very dangerous thing. Clergy and laity alike knew just enough about biblical criticism, the evolutionary controversies of the nineteenth century around Darwin and all that kind of thing, and the decoding processes of popular psychology in the hands particularly of Freud, to have lost their nerve about the true authority of scripture, church doctrine and the life of faith. They seemed sadly to be left with only two alternatives: flabby fashionable

7

liberalism in the name of open-mindedness on the one hand, or an unquestioned fundamentalism on the other. The battle for faith in the middle ground had been temporarily lost, and that is a serious and dangerous moment in the history of religion in general and Christianity in particular.

3. Theology and God-talk

These and many other ingredients have led to a fragmentation in our day at just the very point where religion in faith and practice should bring wholeness and a convergence of human experience. The age-old battle between sacred and secular, physical and spiritual, earth and heaven is once again all too apparent in much contemporary religious presentation. Through many contemporary eyes, the created order, the body, material possessions and institutional power, are at one and the same time objects of abuse and obsession to be indulged as well as objects of derisive distrust to be fled and ignored. The result is a kind of schizophrenia in which spiritualism, unrooted in the material world, clean and disinfected from political, economic and social concern parades as the pure gospel, passing by the economic, political and social needs and concerns of the world 'on the other side' while greed and grief, suppression and suffering go unchecked and unchallenged. With a kind of Swiss-Family-Robinson mentality, the new fundamentalist sects promise an unending supply of their spiritual desert-islands in order that the spiritually minded ('the chosen') may get away from it all. For anyone with a knowledge of religious history, the diagnosis is not difficult. This is none other than that age-old and frequently recurring disease of gnosticism; and once again it was Jung, in his spiritual awareness, who in the early part of the twentieth century pointed to the inevitable emergence of this kind of gnosticism throughout the world. 'The spiritual currents of the present have, in fact, a deep affinity with gnosticism . . . The modern movement which is most impressive numerically is undoubtedly theosophy, together with its continental sister anthroposophy; these are pure gnosticism in a Hindu dress.

Compared with these movements the interest in scientific psychology is negligible.'[9]

Furthermore, such gnostic movements with their ambiguous attitude to 'the world' and 'the flesh' have in practice fired the many charismatic renewal movements of our own day. There is much in these charismatic renewal movements, as we shall see later, which has brought genuine and substantial new life to the Christian Churches. This author would certainly wish to go on record as someone who is lastingly thankful in his own faith for much which the charismatic influence has brought to the witness and vitality of many Churches throughout the world. Nevertheless, at the same time, it has to be admitted that many charismatic renewals are conspicuous in their actual geographical location and are to be found in just the very areas where political issues are at their most acute and most complex (for example in South Africa). In some charismatic over-simplification there is strong evidence of that dangerous doctrine which prescribes the slick palliative of the aspirin of religious experience as a substitute for the more costly medicine of a real involvement with the needs of the world or active compassion for human suffering. Genuine spirituality must for the Christian be earthed, immediate and local and not be seen as another sort of life, always at one stage removed. For the Christian, spirituality and a spiritual life are the way of seeing the *whole* of life in a new and fuller perspective. Sadly, we so often speak of the spiritual life as though it were an alternative life lived in an alternative world, with its own language and its own furniture and fittings. Certainly, for Christians, such a schizoid and fragmented view of the universe is unthinkable. There is a man in heaven because first there was God on the earth, and both are one and the same person whom we call Jesus. Henceforth, heaven and earth are now 'full of his glory' for those with 'eyes to see' and 'ears to hear'. The spiritual life, or the inner life, is the training of the eyes and the ears and indeed of every other faculty of the human personality to be sensitive to this glory at every turn in our journey of exploration in earth, on earth, through earth and into heaven. 'In his hands are *all* the corners of the earth.'[10] The implications of that sort of faith are staggering and revolutionary and mark a distinctive turning point in the history of religious experience. As we shall see later in the book for the religion of the incarnation there can be no corner of the earth for Christians which is not 'in His hands' waiting to be moulded afresh and to recover again the shape and features of its creator. Such is the work to which prayer and spirituality commit the Christian and with which that same prayer and spirituality are inseparably bound.[11]

4. The dangers of religion

Yet such a statement begs the very question with which we shall be concerned at every turn of the page in this book. It is precisely the shape and features of the creator which we need to know if our religion is to be real and our God talk is to ring true and be responsible. It is that most difficult and dangerous word, 'god', again which rears its head; and so it always has been since the beginning of time and so it always will be till the end of time. It is mankind's first and last word. At some new moment of discovery, or some breakthrough in human achievement, we reach for this word in our vocabulary: it is the alpha and omega of every new and breath-taking experience. At the last breath also, either individually or in some corporate holocaust, again we shall reach for this word in our vocabulary: it is the omega and end of all human yearnings and experience. 'Oh, God!' Yet what does this word mean? What meaning can we or dare we give to it? For the danger is always the same, namely, that we shall give to this word, 'god', just and only the meaning which most comfortably fits *our* needs and *our* insights. We shall begin to sketch in the features of this unknown and unseen God, but sadly they will be all too easily merely a replica of our own – a projection of our own unfulfilled desires, aspirations and hopes. We make God in our own image – a tin god, on the contemporary supermarket of all other do-it-yourself amateurisms. It is the oldest habit in the world: in a word it is called idolatry. 'If God created us in his own image, we have more than reciprocated.'[12]

10

In Jewish law, the commandment was quite explicit: 'You shall not make for yourself any graven image or any likeness'.[13] You can forbid men and women to do that on stone or canvas or any other obvious media of the art forms, but you will not stop them from committing idolatry in their hearts and in their minds. It is the disease and danger of all religion which no law in itself can eradicate. For what we need to admit freely at the outset of this book, and indeed throughout all religious discussions, is that 'God-talk' is as dangerous as it is inevitable. In one sense all serious-thinking human beings talk theology at some point in their lives, and equally at some point set themselves up as theologians. How often in a hospital ward will a patient stoically utter the words: 'Well, I suppose it's all sent to try us'. Those words are theology – bad theology but nevertheless theology! According to this sort of theology God is the sort of God, apparently, who sends illness and disease 'to try us'. What an extraordinary picture of God, yet possibly nearer to the theology of the man in the street than most parsons would dare to believe. And such popular impressions of God are legion – all crying out for a new direction, pastoral care and oversight, education and further information. Such is the task of living theology at the heart of the Church. The Church always needs a sturdy and searching theology, and never more than when tides and waves of religious revivals are flowing, unquestioned and unchecked.

For the danger is that we shall be tempted to think that all amateur theology is harmless enough until we bump into the contemporary heresy, for example, of apartheid, or recall at another chapter in history the theological implications behind the rise of Nazism in the thirties of this century. Both apartheid and Nazism sprang from wrong theology. They are based on belief that God is the sort of God who created some people with particular coloured skins or certain blood in them (as with the Jews) as *inferior* to others. Theology begets belief and belief begets behaviour. Bad theology begets bad beliefs and before long such beliefs beget evil behaviour: evil because our religious convictions or our theology go very deep indeed in the human psyche and create

11

stronger motivations and more powerful prejudices than any other driving force within man: evil because, when the best goes wrong it is the worst (and not just a little mistaken): evil, because religion gone wrong is never just a little misguided, but always claims infallibility, total sincerity and the un-willingness to bring its assumptions to the bar of reason, discussion and probing. Many more evils in the world than we realize are derived from religious convictions and bad theology. Every tyrant in the world has known that you do not start by trying to get people to *do* wicked things and fight wicked wars. You start by brainwashing them into believing wrong things and always forge the signature of God as the ultimate authority underwriting those wrong beliefs. Then all hell is let loose, literally, for you have harnessed the most powerful motivations of all to do evil things in the name of the good – 'your god'.

At its best it was this insight which led the medieval Church to be more concerned about wrong beliefs than about wrong actions. The *Canterbury Tales* are totally free from prudish concern about the ordinary everyday sins of ordinary everyday men and women, for it knew that ordinary everyday sinners and sins are readily forgivable – every day! The medieval Church was clearly exceptionally (some might say excessively) concerned about the propagation of wrong belief (as it saw it) and heresy (as it called it) because it realized that an epidemic of heresy (half truth) would soon lead to evil behaviour in the name of God. Many of the hair-splitting arguments at medieval dinner parties may seem very trivial to us today and are frequently rather patronizingly represented as trivial arguments about angels on heads of pins. Yet, in fact, they were based on a real concern for the health of society at the most profound of all levels: the level of belief, theology and religious conviction. It is sad that more of the energies of our contemporary churches are not given to combatting wrong *belief* about apartheid, the responsibility for wealth, and the right love of the body and other contemporary causes, rather than band-waggoning with quasi-moralistic marches and protests. For the battle must always be primarily for the minds and hearts of men and women, where belief and conviction go deep and where the features and face of God are slowly being formed or deformed.

So at this point it is important to re-establish, hopefully with clarity, the premise which clearly is in need of frequent and forceful reiteration, namely, that religion is seldom harmless, always potentially dangerous and perhaps never more so than when it is conquering and going forth to conquer. That does not – and indeed it must not – lead us to a wrong temperance in religious matters, nor to a cool and urbane attitude to our inner life and the claims of religious discipleship and total commitment. But it does lay upon religious leaders a solemn and subtle vocation to be equally deeply committed to education, teaching and learning and making sure that these are conspicuous as disciplines within all discipleship. Responsible 'God-talk' or good theology must be the programme of all the Churches at the present time, and the activity of the whole people of God: particularly the responsibility of the specialists and professionals but certainly not exclusively their property. The healthy environment of all religious conviction must be a living theology and in the best sense a popular theology, and it is to such a task that this book unapologetically addresses itself on the particular front of Anglicanism and its claims and aims within world-wide Christianity.

In all of this, theology and theologians (hopefully in that order) will also have a stall in the market place of differing world religions and among the Churches and denominations of Christianity. This book is not intended as a highly professional theological apology for one particular Church in the arena of Christianity, and it is certainly not an attempt at salesmanship for a particular brand of religious adherence. It is an attempt to speak to a need and to respond to an opportunity. There is a new opportunity for God-talk at the present time: there is a renewed quest for faith and belief and, therefore, a new need for clear signposts and helpful landmarks at a time when many are experiencing a shifting of the sands and an earthquake in the rocks and foundations of the heart and soul of man. But the opportunity and the need go together. We need to help ordinary men and women to have the tools, the maps, the compass and the ropes with which best to free them for the opportunity of exploration into faith and into God. It is to that task that we turn in the name, it is true, of Anglicanism – but hopefully with a wider brief and with greater expectations. The exercise of the next few chapters is not for an elite: it is an open invitation to an exercise (admittedly strenuous) which like all exercise is related to good shape and good health, in an age when not a few are sadly deformed even in the name of faith, and in which new tyrannies and fears are conspicuous where freedom and faith should be gloriously working hand in hand. It is the conviction of this book that Anglicanism within Christianity has a particular part to play in such an exercise.

NOTES

1. *The Collected Works of C. G. Jung*, Volume 10, paragraph 167, Routledge & Kegan Paul, 1964
2. Alvin Toffler, *The Third Wave*, p. 32, Pan Books, 1980
3. Ibid. p. 376
4. Ibid. p. 300
5. Ibid. p. 320
6. Ibid. p. 321
7. Ibid. p. 409
8. St Luke 21.26
9. *The Collected Works of C. G. Jung*, Volume 10, paragraph 169
10. Psalm 95.4
11. viz. chapter 6
12. Voltaire, *Le Sottisier*
13. Exodus 20.4

2. The shape of faith

1. The need for a theological renewal today

In the last chapter, we have seen something of the opportunities and needs in our contemporary religious climate – at least in the west. It would be wrong to be negative or over cautious at moments like this in history when, once again, talk of God and everything from religious discussions to large parochial teaching missions are much more in vogue than they have been for some time. The writer of this book is gratefully aware, through his own frequent broadcasting, how very much the climate has changed – especially in the media, where the small protected 'God slots' of the fifties and sixties have grown and expanded until religion and religious affairs are no longer the poor relative in the family of various concerns and programmes either on radio or television. There is more coverage for religion in general and Christianity in particular, at least in the United Kingdom, especially on radio and television, though also generally in paperbacks, magazines and newspapers. Talk about God, prayer and 'spiritual things' today, and you will always have an audience.

But equally, of course, talk about black magic, tarot cards, spiritualism, healing, your stars, or exorcism and you will certainly have an audience. The media frequently invites us to do so. Thank God – it is an opportunity! I for one will use any platform or invitation to get a hearing for the Christian faith – presumably that was something of what Paul meant when he urged the pastors of those new first century churches to speak the word, 'in season and out of season'.[1] In the market place – and on ordinary bookstalls and bookstands, or even on station platforms – 'religion' (in the good and bad meaning of that word) has its slot and appears to be able to hold its own in the hard world of commercialism. But now it is more important than ever before, perhaps, for the customer to be educated and delivered from inevitable bewilderment as he seeks to shop around this expanding market. All that glitters is not gold.

Things are not what they seem to be. There is a pressing need for market research by the 'professionals' and for educated awareness on the part of the customers. This book is primarily directed towards the latter.

In a word theology matters. The crisis in all the Churches and in all religions is a theological crisis – it is to do with belief and conviction. No amount of God-experience, however rich and releasing, will in itself be enough; and certainly in this area of human endeavour, sincerity is supremely never enough. It is always the simplistic failing of materialistic man, to suppose that in material matters it is always best to send for the expert, while in spiritual matters, of course, the enthusiastic and sincere amateur will do. Nothing could be further from the truth. In fact it is the very opposite of the truth. In materialistic matters, the enthusiastic and sincere amateur often gets it right by short cuts and instinct (half the gardens and allotments in England clearly flourish at the hands of such amateurs, to say nothing of do-it-yourself decorators, car mechanics and home carpenters). It is in spiritual matters and the skills of the mind and the spirit of man, that there is no substitute for the expert. The only difference is that today, in an expanding market of faith, religion and things of the spirit, every lay man and lay woman really does need to know some theology and to be articulate about their faith – to know their way around this market. While such knowledge will need to draw upon their hearts and their deep inner experiences and convictions it must also be infused and informed by what Justin Martyr used to call 'a flame in the mind'. It was Cardinal Newman who said, well over a century ago, 'I want an articulate and well educated laity'. But a great deal has happened since the sober days of Cardinal Newman, and today the need for an articulate and theologically aware Church is more pressing and urgent than ever. Today's world is a world of instant opinions and packaged discussions, processed for the millions and reaching to the inner ear and eye of the public at a rate and to an extent that Cardinal Newman and his nineteenth century contemporaries could never have foreseen. Furthermore, this process is still accelerating and further

16

compounded by the new techniques of computer communication. There will be no difficulty in communicating the message and massaging it for precise and local needs at every level and piping it into the homes and hearts of millions in every language across the globe by the end of the century. The question will still remain – though it might well become more pressing as time goes on – what is the message and how can we equip men and women with the necessary intellectual and spiritual fibre to resist the slick and immediate, the half truth and the skilfully confectioned lie about life and death, love and God, time and eternity? Mass manipulation is increasingly the climate of our age and if that age is in some sense to be a religious age, as it appears it will almost certainly be, then we should not be surprised to discover that such manipulation will extend into this most rich and dangerous area of humanity's experience.

2. The need for lay participation in the theological life of the Churches

For this reason, if for no other, there is an urgent need for a theological renewal in all the Churches today. By that, however, we do not mean a multiplication of professional chairs of theology in colleges and universities. Bishops and clergy must begin again to talk and preach theology: in a word to talk about God. The environment of the Church must become charged again with theological vitality, but a theology which is prepared to draw not only on the Bible and the tradition and teaching of the Church (important though both are and shockingly neglected though they have both been in recent history). The theological life and climate of the Church will come alive when it is clothed in the flesh and blood of the experiences of the market place and the insights of the laboratory. In that sense all good theology in the history of the Church has been 'occasional theology'. That is to say it has arisen from a response to the events and insights of the day. It was, for example, when Rome, the capital of the ancient civilized world, was sacked and pillaged by the barbarians (AD 410), that Augustine of Hippo saw the need to respond to that event and to set it within a world view of history and to see it as part of his theological vision of the direction and purpose of history. That is occasional theology. It is always the best sort of theology, claiming no protective market or specialization for itself but rather meeting a vivid and vital need of the day and bringing to bear upon it the perspective of the gospel and the kingdom of God. It will hardly be surprising that in such circumstances as these, the lay contribution will have a vital part to play. It will not be patronized as a second-class token consideration; but rather, it will supply the mud and straw for the twentieth century equivalent of everything which at one time made up the straw in the manger, the wood of the cross, the census of Quirinius, or the political conflict between Herod and Pilate as the raw material of the first incarnation of Christ two thousand years ago. For then, and then only, theology receives the vitality which can never be dodged and the challenge which can never go unheeded as once again the word is made flesh and dwells among us. Theology will be a true extension of that incarnation – 'Christmas comes once more'. It will also be a further explosion of Pentecost and we shall all hear again in our 'own language' the wonderful works of God. Such is the continuing task of theology and that is why it is the discipline of the whole people of God and not just of the academic theologians or the professional clergy. Of course there will always be a place in the disciplines (as in all disciplines) for the specialist. But as in medicine, health is not the property of the specialist but rather the pursuit and concern of all, so in theology, God-talk is not the property of the specialist few, but rather the pursuit and concern of the whole people of God. However, we must go further than that.

For Christian theology is the cuckoo of the disciplines and lays all its best eggs in other people's nests! It is precisely because the laity are frequently in charge, or involved in those other nests (often conspicuous as those who have built them in the first place), that their contribution is so vital. After all, it is their natural habitat – the place where they work and the place where in a real sense they are at home. Here we are speaking of the laity, however, and we should not necessarily confuse them with those whom we have come to regard as church men and church women: the sort who are seriously in danger today of spending all their spare time in synods and church committees and who are designated, quite irresponsibly, as 'representing' the laity. There is always the danger that they will be about as unrepresentative as they possibly could be. Generally speaking, they are still predominantly from one class in society, the other side of sixty (and perhaps that is generous) and nearly always women. (This is not surprising, in a Church like the Anglican Church, where there are four times more women in church than men!) No – that is not what we mean by the role of the laity in the theological life of the church. The lay contribution is not democracy's answer to an over clericalized Church. It stems from a need which theology in itself has to contain within its own debate the dialectic between God's word in the scriptures and in the Church (the business of redemption) and God's word in creation and the natural world around us. Those whose work and skills, insights and experiences are mainly drawn from the everyday life of creation and the world are best equipped to earth and clothe that word of God in redemption, forming one whole Christian witness. The word will always require flesh if we are to behold it and respond to it – witness to it and draw attention to it. It will not come to us neat, otherwise it will not be a word of the kingdom, but rather the jargon words of ecclesiastical ghettos and churchy concerns. For in fact we are speaking of the kingdom of God (and not simply the Church of God) as the place and environment for this theological commitment and insight in which all Christians have a part to play. Such then will be the theological environment of Christian inquiry.

For in the end the biblical specialist and the church historian, for example, cannot in a real sense do theology in isolation. Their specializations are only the tools in a larger process. The process must involve a third party, but a third party who is not regarded and certainly need not necessarily be simply a second class amateur, but rather one who holds his own as a third specialist in this more subtle way of pursuing

God-talk or theology. He or she will have dug deep and looked long into various aspects of the world's experiences, where the word of God is always at work and where something of his features and purposes are also discernible. So it will be that theological debate will always be tripartite: the word of God in scripture; the word of God in the tradition and teaching of the Church and also the word of God hidden within the very fibre of his creation. The genius of a living theology will be to see how these 'three witnesses' can 'agree'.[2] For creation and continuing creation will always have a special witness to bring to the bar of theology since in Christian thought we do not believe that God has in one divine fiat created the world and that his handiwork is now complete. Our understanding is that creation is a continuing process within which there is the further revelation and purpose which we have come to call redemption. That continuing redemptive process is set within a continuing creative process in which man at some point comes to play a vital and determinative part. The well-known text from Isaiah in many excellent translations is sadly and wrongly rendered in the past historic tense, as though creation is something that God has done and finished with. The well-known passage from Isaiah is thus rendered in most translations as follows: 'Thus says God, the Lord, who created the heavens and stretched them out, who spread forth the earth and what comes from it, who gives breath to the people upon it and spirit to those who walk in it.'[3] In fact it should be accurately rendered in the continuing present tense and would read dramatically as follows: 'Thus says God, the Lord, who is creating the heavens and stretching them out, and who is spreading forth the earth and what comes from it, who is giving breath to the people upon it and spirit to those who walk in it'. The so-called lay contribution draws its strength – or should do – from its daily involvement in precisely that continuing process of God's continuing creation, in which man has a vital and indispensable part. Every discipline of human life should lead its faithful disciples to the very threshold of glory, if what Christians frequently say in their Eucharist is really the truth – 'heaven and earth are full' of

God's glory. The other end of the microscope or the telescope, the other end of the surgeon's knife or the laser beam is territory which cannot be simply written off as merely of human concern or simply as the secular world, by anyone worthy of the name of being human. For, in fact, it finds its true significance when it is related to the evidence and witness of redemption as an echo of another word: the word of God in Jesus Christ revealed in scripture and the teaching of the Church. So it is that 'deep calls to deep', and in its life and resonance there is a word, a single word derived from three evidences or three words. Such is living theology – God-talk. It is the word and the words which emerge out of that kind of theology which will give that dangerous word 'God' its full meaning and its true face. It shares something of the same great vision of Irenaeus, a bishop in Gaul at the end of the second century who used to speak of the word 'accustoming' himself to mankind and mankind to himself.

Sometimes we see this process primarily as 'making connections'. For example, suffering which has been nobly endured by a person is suddenly seen and *experienced* as related to and connected with the word of God in scripture in a passage like the suffering servant in the book of the prophet Isaiah or the book of Job, and also with the undeserved suffering of Jesus. Meaningless suffering, nobly born, suddenly (or gradually) becomes meaningful and redemptive and can even be borne as creative and purposeful. In quite a different key, patterns of behaviour and reversal observed in cell structure, animals, or in a novel will begin to connect with and illuminate that reversal which we call resurrection, not only in the fortunes of the people of the Old Testament and in their corporate history, not only in the death and resurrection events of Jesus in the New Testament, nor even also in the acting out of this and showing forth of all this in the liturgy of the Church. It will be seen as nothing less than the woof and warp of the whole texture of life at every level. Death and resurrection will be written into the very fibre of human experience,[4] as surely as when 'a grain of wheat falls into the earth'[5] it must die in order to bring forth new life, or as surely as 'when a woman is in travail she has sorrow' but 'when she is delivered of the child she no longer remembers the anguish, for the joy that a child is born into the world'.[6] So it is, that faith will now no longer be a matter of swallowing a number of facts of faith, but rather a way of seeing the whole of life and life as whole. It will bring a true unity to all our human understandings and insights – that true unity which is something much larger than ecclesiastical ecumenism.

Barbara Ward speaks of this when she writes: 'We have lacked a wider rationale of unity. Our prophets have sought it. Our poets have dreamed of it. But it is only in our own day that astronomers, physicists, geologists, chemists, biologists, anthropologists and ethnologists have all combined in a single witness of advanced science to tell us that, in every alphabet of our being, we do indeed belong, to a single system, powered by a single energy, manifesting a fundamental unity under all its variations, depending for its survival on the balance and health of the total system.'[7]

Of course this process is not likely to hit the hysteria of the headlines, nor is it likely to be processed and packaged easily for the mass media. Neither, on the other hand, is it to say that the process should lead to obscurantism for its own sake, or to such a specialist way of seeing things that it is restricted only to the privileged few. On the contrary it is a fairly certain test that the person who cannot speak the truth simply has not really understood it. Much of what has passed for intellectualism and higher learning has surrounded itself often with the myth of jargon, and certainly theology and theologians have excelled themselves in this direction. For surely those who have taught us most about God have spoken in simple and direct language. It was Barth, that truly great theologian who, when he was asked if he could summarize in a sentence the content of his twenty years writing in his huge work *Church Dogmatics*, turned to the well-known Sunday School chorus and said that it could all be summarized in the two lines – 'Jesus loves me this I know, because the Bible tells me so'. Such is the simplicity of which great theology is made. That is not to say, however, that we should give the impression that we have got it all buttoned up. The great Christian guru must always keep his disciples travelling and always point them away from themselves (and from himself) through the known and the articulate words to the unknown and the ineffable word of God. Good, lively contemporary and occasional theology is a healthy environment of faith and is the urgent antidote to the ready-made, simplistic and fringe churches and sects of our own day.

For it is the hole created by the theological vacuum of the mainstream Churches which so many of the sects and religious cults are filling, and in its turn this is a judgement upon those Churches. The crisis is a theological crisis and it will be met only by a fresh understanding of the importance and place of theology in the life and faith of the whole people of God. This understanding of theology will have a place for the specialist, while refusing on the one hand to be dominated by the specialist and on the other hand equally refusing to be wrongly apprehensive of such skills and insights in the name of a kind of triumphalist amateurism. Such an understanding of theology will make demands on the intellect but it will speak also to the whole arena of human experience at its deepest and will not be tyrannized by the mind and the cerebral process or excommunicated by the intellectual expert. This theology will be expanded always by the bishops, clergy and professional theologians, but it will not be exclusively their property. It will belong to the whole people of God, because it will be derived from the insights of all – a true *consensus fidelium*. It will include the witness and evidence of the word of God in his creation and not least in the natural sciences, with which it will also seek a resonance as well as with the other evidences of the scriptures and the traditions of the Church. Such theology will be expressed and tested in the climate of prayer, worship and the everyday life of faith, ruthlessly diverting the attention of its disciples away from the Church to the ultimate demands of the kingdom of God. In every sense therefore the need of all the Churches in an age of religious awakening is the urgent need for a profound theological renewal.

3. The place of Anglican theology and the method of Anglican theology

In this context we may well ask: 'What then is the specific contribution of Anglicanism and in what ways can this comparatively small section of the Christian Churches make its voice heard in the whole debate about theological renewal?' Anglicanism is certainly small (almost minute numerically) when compared with the great western Church of Rome or the huge Churches of the Eastern Orthodox world. Furthermore, by its history, its influence has tended to be largely limited to the English speaking world of the nineteenth century British Empire which has therefore necessarily limited its influence among other cultures and its real contact with other major world religions. Even within the ranks of Anglicanism, its affiliations between the present provinces and member Churches of the Anglican Communion throughout the world are rather loose and tenuous, to say the least, claiming only some kind of undefined loyalty with and relation to the ancient See of Canterbury. In world Christianity and in the forum of world faith, what place will Anglicanism really hold? At some point in this book we shall need to strike a note of realism about the size and influence of Anglicanism in world religion and in world Christianity. However, for the moment, our emphasis is upon the distinctive characteristics of Anglicanism in an attempt to discover what it has to offer to the other Churches and indeed to other faiths at the level of its distinctive theological method. For we must certainly recall that the thesis of this book is no attempt to sell the Anglican Church as a thing-in-itself. If it were, it would be little better than an appeal for a new and latter-day British Empire in terms of religious affiliation: come back the Empire, all is forgiven! The influence and contribution of Anglicanism at the present time is not of that order at all. 'For while the Anglican church', writes Bishop Michael Ramsey, 'is vindicated by its place in history, with a strikingly balanced witness to Gospel and Church and sound learning, its greater vindication lies in its pointing through its own history to something of which it is a fragment. Its credentials are its incompleteness, with the tension and the travail in its soul. It is clumsy and untidy, it baffles neatness and logic. For it is sent not to commend itself as "the best type of Christianity", but by its very brokenness to point to the universal Church wherein all have died'.[8] Surely in the present pursuit for Christian unity, all Churches are increasingly aware of what they lack and furthermore, we are at last beginning to realize that no one Church as it stands at the moment has that pleroma and fullness of gospel catholicity which we believe Christ longs to give to his Church. So many reformations and counter reformations and renewals in the history of the Church have brought about further fragmentation. So often Christians in their history have only found it possible to affirm one aspect of truth while rejecting other aspects of truth. Roughly – though something of an over-simplification – this process of fragmentation would lead us to see three main emphases at work throughout the history of the Church. Sadly each has brought about its own fragmentation when it has been over-emphasized at various points throughout history.

In the first place there has been a section of Christians who have set the scriptures above all other evidence in their theology. *'Sola scriptura'* was very much the cry of the Reformation Protestant Churches. In those Churches, the scriptures have become so elevated above other emphases and evidences in theology that many would claim that such Churches are besieged between the two outer covers of the Bible, petrified and fossilized, unable to grow and develop, static and lacking that dynamic which is a true sign of any living organism. In these Churches there has been a recurring tendency towards fundamentalism and literalism in the scriptures and a desire to give an infallible authority to scripture in every word and sentence. This has often led to individualistic interpretation of scripture and to an almost magical and superstitious use of the scriptures. Much American Christianity in the 'Bible belt' is flavoured with just this kind of Christian witness – a witness which is frequently legalistic and also incidentally strongly Old Testament in its moral teaching.

The second emphasis is the emphasis which gives exclusive weight to the tradition, teaching and sacramental life of the Church, frequently in danger of placing it above scripture and claiming an authority for the dogma of the Church in catholic circles very similar, though different in kind, to the fundamentalism that the Protestants would claim for the Bible and the word of God as it is revealed in scripture. Again, this emphasis in isolation, leads to a static understanding of the nature of the Church with a subsequent hardening of the arteries: the catholic cardiac condition! It degenerates (as with biblical fundamentalism) into a rigidity and legalism, but in this case the emphasis is upon the minutiae of catholic practice in worship, liturgy, prayer and the Christian life. In a strange way, both the isolation of scripture and the isolation of the traditions of the Church, wherever they become closed systems, while standing conventionally at opposite ends of the spectrum of the Church, do in practice tend to appeal to a similar temperament: the temperament which can only live with certainty; the cautious fearful temperament, which cannot cope with inner conflict or blurred edges to the argument and which mistakenly believes that unless something or someone is totally infallible they have no authority. It is significant that Cardinal Newman oscillated in his life from the extremes of evangelicalism to the shelter of the Roman Catholic Church with its apparent certainties and its tidy arguments. Appeals to certainty, infallibility and unquestioned authority always receive a ready hearing in times of uncertainty and instability and where there is chorused abroad a fear for what is coming on the earth or to individual temperaments who are largely motivated by fear. All alike tend to seek security through certainty or to see in conflict only concession and weakness. We can be totalitarian in our religious allegiances even more easily than we can be totalitarian in our politics. The appeal to unanimity, uniformity and streamlined certainty will have a recurring vogue in history and not least at times like our own when, as we have seen in the earlier chapters, it is the fundamentalist and sharp-featured Churches at both ends of the spectrum which are apparently (numerically at least) most effective in our own day and recruiting large numbers of disciples.

The third ingredient in the Christian theological emphasis is at best a genuine antidote to the two emphases outlined above. Sometimes it goes under the name of modernist or liberal – neither of which are particularly apt labels. This emphasis in theological witness and God-talk, wishes to emphasize the place of human experience and the witness of the word of God and the hand of God in his creation in precisely the kind of way that we have outlined earlier in this chapter. It is ready to listen to the evidence of science (especially to the natural sciences). It sees the place of reason and human exploration and speculation. It gives strong value to man as made in the image of God and the creation as mirroring (however dimly) the features and purposes of the creator. It is ready to hear all this evidence in the realm of human speculation even if it seems to conflict with the evidence of revelation in scripture and the traditional teachings of the Church. Far from being anxious and perturbed by conflicting truths or untidy edges, it almost exalts this and sees it as a safer sign of truth, being distrustful of neatly packaged truth and even appalled at claims of infallibility and certainty. It sees the truth of Christ as essentially dynamic and developing, slowly unfolding, and the place of the disciple as essentially a pilgrim (like the wise men of old) following the star through conflict and contradiction, refusing to stand still and claim for any authority – be it the Bible or the Church – a permanent and ultimate definition of God who is essentially *beyond* all our deepest thoughts and all our most generous formulae. Such a spirit of continuing enquiry in approach to theology and dogma is perhaps most aptly summed up in the words of A. F. Balfour:

Our highest truths are but half-truths,
Think not to settle down for ever in any truth.
Make use of it as a tent in which to pass a summer's night,
But build no house in it, or it will be your tomb.
When you first have an inkling of its insufficiency

And begin to descry a dim counter-truth coming up
  beyond
Then weep not, but give thanks:
It is the Lord's voice, whispering, "Take up thy bed and
  walk".[9]

Of course such a position is widely open to caricature as being fuzzy at the edges and woolly within: a compromise or the soft-option for the disciple who always wishes to hold back from total commitment. It is true that often those who have held this 'liberal' position have fallen to the temptation of idolizing the intellect and isolating the cerebral processes of human experience from all other equally valid experiences and insights. Furthermore, such an emphasis has frequently led to individualism and a distrust of corporate faith.

Within this tradition we need to trace at least two differing emphases: on the one hand there is the emphasis which places the intellect as the ultimate arbiter and which speaks of reason and makes its appeal exclusively to reason. On the other hand, there is also the emphasis which places some emotional experience or movement of the heart and sees this as the ultimate arbiter. This would and can include the charismatic experiences of religious faith, the stirrings of the heart and emotions. It must be said in praise of both reason and experience that they loosen up the rigidity of revelation where the evidence is restricted only to the teaching of the Bible or the Church. It bends what is rigid, it warms what can become frigid. But in itself this third way, left unchecked by the other two, can also become rigid and restricting, fundamentalist and authoritarian. In practice, in either of its forms – whether the tyranny of reason or the tyranny of some emotional experience – there is a tendency to produce a highly individualistic approach to religion which pits that individual experience whether it be of the conscience or the intellectual insight of the individual, against the teachings of the scriptures or the teachings of the Church by claiming to be 'on the same wave-length' as God. Inevitably such people will frequently be ill at ease in the organized life of any of the mainstream Churches. The Quak-

28

ers, in many ways, reflect something of this witness: distrustful of dogma and cautious about church structure or ecclesiastical affiliations, they have borne witness to that inner experience of God which, although widely open to misuse, abuse and distortion, is none the less a precious and important ingredient in any living theology and any authentic witness to a living God, making himself known to and experienced by humankind. It is perhaps worth noting in passing that Quakers have spoken to two rather differing aspects in Christian spirituality throughout their history: the prayer of silence and religion of the heart, which at various points in their experience has released people from the tyrannies of an over-structured worship and has sometimes even been accompanied by 'quaking' and physical expressions of release. Equally Quakers have been conspicuous in their ministry to the mind and have made a strong appeal to university and college environments, frequently speaking out in a prophetic way on matters of social concern and contemporary ethical issues.

In all of this, we have seen that at the heart of all theology there is an essential dialectic – a dialectic which is conspicuously inherent in the human spirit. It is precisely the dialectic at the heart of all knowledge and all human understanding. It breaks down roughly as follows: revelation versus speculation: dogmatic as opposed to apophatic: objective and subjective: imposed from without versus what is embraced from within. On earth – and this side of heaven – these will always appear to be opposites and will always be hard to reconcile. They will tempt us to take up arms to fight the caricature of the opposing spirit (which is in fact within each one of us and is in some sense our own 'shadow'). Yet if we do so we shall damage ourselves, for both in fact are part of the human need and the human experience, and in the end we shall see that both alike are derived from the one God who is both within and yet finally beyond; who has made himself known through the finite world yet is unknowable in his infinity; whose ultimate purposes belong to eternity, yet who has revealed himself in the particularity of time, place and a person; who is the word in each and every created being and yet whose conclusive word is Jesus, made flesh, revealed and born on earth yet reigning ultimately in heaven.

4. Renewal in a fullness of theology and life

The pleroma or fullness of the Church, towards which all Churches are drawn, must be a Church which will seek to make of these two apparently opposite and irreconcilable attributes one whole person. The truly ecumenical vision of our age is the quest in all the Churches for the reappropriation of bits and pieces which have broken down and broken off throughout history, but which now are being raised-up and re-evaluated as parts of the fuller and richer whole. Such is the vision of the truly ecumenical spirit at work at the close of the twentieth century, across large parts of the Christian Churches.

There are signs of this fullness already at work. Perhaps most notable of these was the strategic breakthrough of the Roman Catholic Church at the Second Vatican Council. Since the Counter-Reformation, the Roman Catholic Church had in practice tended to exalt the place of tradition above the place of the witness and evidence of scripture. Yet it was in the historic proceedings of the Council that Pope John XXIII intervened at one point to emphasize a radical realignment between the evidence of scripture and the evidence of tradition inviting the former to come up higher and sit on a basis of equal authority with the latter as colleagues. From now onwards, revelation has a 'double source' (Bible *and* tradition) and the theology and God-talk of the Roman Church has been radically revised as it finds itself to be the end result of an *equal* obedience both to scripture and to tradition. This was a major and monumental breakthrough in the history of Christian witness. We can of course point to all other kinds of equally obvious signs of change of heart and mind throughout all the Churches in their theology and in the life and worship of their members. It is hard to put labels on Christians in quite the way we used to do. Slogans have softened and badges are less trustworthy. We find ourselves being continually sur-

30

prised by the spirituality and thoughts behind the badges and the labels. In practice the spirituality of the Roman Catholic Church has become far more scriptural. The laity take a larger part in the worship and life of the Church; there is more singing in the liturgy and a more pastoral emphasis in the application of the sacrament of Penance (in which there is a strong element of scripture). Furthermore there is a real sense of joy and peace in much corporate catholic life and worship. In practice it is almost as though the Roman Catholic Church has taken on something of the spirit of Methodism together with a bit of the Salvation Army and the Reformed Churches and rolled them all into one! There is a fullness, a richness and a diversity which all other Christians must witness with gratitude and with profound thanksgiving to God.

Equally the Reformation Churches have taken a fresh look at so much which at one time would have been regarded as popish and repugnant. The Eucharist has been reappropriated as the characteristic act of worship for reformation Christians. The place of episcopacy is under favourable review by those Churches which abandoned it at the Reformation. All around us there is a new willingness to look behind the party labels and to see values in customs of worship and sacramental life, biblical spirituality and methods of prayer – all of which had been ruled out of order as either unscriptural, untraditional or unreasonable at various points in the history and fragmentation of the Christian Churches. All this represents a remarkable – almost radical – new recipe and readjustment, and two particular Churches are worthy perhaps of special mention as being particularly conspicuous in witnessing to such a fuller life and pleroma. It is noteworthy that many Churches in the west are discovering for themselves the particular calibre of the Orthodox Churches of the east. In their particular theological structure there has always been a remarkable ability to hold together what we in the west have separated, precisely because the Orthodox Churches have always been eager to approach theology from both ends: dogmatic and apophatic. They have been wonderfully rescued from many of the dangers in the western Churches which arose from an unbalanced emphasis on dogma — whether through scripture or the Church. They have held together the dialectic which is ready alike to say what God is (dogmatic) and also at the same time to say what God is not (apophatic). Such a balance will be of strategic significance in all ecumenical encounters in the coming years. It has never made for tidiness in Orthodox theology, but it has rescued the Churches of the east from some of the worst abuses of dogmatism which have caused so much trouble in the west and which have been all too obvious and all too divisive at various points of our history both in the Churches of the Reformation and also in the mainstream western Church of Rome.

Alongside the Eastern Churches, Anglicanism takes its place and it is in this setting that we are now ready to evaluate the particular witness of Anglicanism. Archbishop William Temple wrote: 'Our special character and, as we believe, our peculiar contribution to the universal Church, arises from the fact that, owing to historic circumstances, we have been enabled to combine in our one fellowship the traditional Faith and Order of the Catholic Church with that immediacy of approach to God through Christ to which the Evangelical Churches especially bear witness, and freedom of intellectual inquiry, whereby the correlation of the Christian revelation and advancing knowledge is constantly effected.'[10] There it is. a threefold witness: three resources by which Anglican theology is tested, tried and developed. The witness of the Church in its teaching, faith and order throughout the centuries; the particular evidence and emphasis of scripture in the historic activity of God in prophecy and law in the Old Testament and in the person of Jesus in the New Testament; and thirdly, God's revelation through his word in the evidence of the consecrated human reason and experience relating 'Christian revelation' and 'advancing knowledge' to each other. It was Bishop Charles Gore who enthusiastically wrote at the end of the nineteenth century: 'I believe with a conviction the strength of which I could hardly express, that it is the vocation' of Anglicanism 'to realize and to offer to mankind a catholicism which is scriptural, and represents the whole of scripture; which is historical, and can know itself free in the face of historical and critical science; which is rational and constitutional in its claims of authority, free at once from lawlessness and imperialism'.[11] Bishop Paget speaks in the same vein: 'For on equal loyalty to the unconflicting rights of reason, of scripture, and of tradition rest the distinctive strength and hope of the English church'.[12] Jeremy Taylor had originally affirmed this threefold cord when he wrote: 'I affirm nothing but upon grounds of scripture, or universal tradition, or right reason discernible by every disinterested person.'[13] Over several centuries the witness to this tripartite method in theology has been consistent in Anglicanism: reason (and all that is related to the deepest and most authentic of human experience); tradition, the witness of the Church as the community of faith throughout the ages; scripture, that record of the people of God, fulfilled in the one who himself is God's chosen revelation and final word – even Jesus Christ.

Such a tripartite claim is latent within all the mainstream churches and yet there are real signs that such an approach is being seen as the explicit goal of many of the Churches in the present day. It represents a richness and a fullness which enables many of the previously divisive elements in Christian faith to have their place without any one element playing the tyrant over the rest. So Dr Alec Vidler writes: 'Anglican theology is true to its genius when it is seeking to reconcile opposed systems, rejecting them as exclusive systems, but showing that the principle for which each stands has its own place within the total orbit of Christian truth, and in the long run is secure only within that orbit or . . . when it is held in tension with other apparently opposed, but really complementary principles'.[14] Of course, as we shall see later in this book, and as we need honestly to admit, such a system does not make for easy life. The tension is real and the temptations are strong to hare off with spectacular devotion after one or other of the three evidences in the name of party strength, commitment or clarity. Equally it is all too easy to turn the tension itself into a cause and in the name of intellectual honesty and comprehensiveness to refuse to come down on any

33

one side in any one argument. We shall have to face up to these and other weaknesses in Anglicanism later in the book. Yet at the outset, perhaps the evidence of these opening chapters might tentatively suggest that Anglicanism could well be 'an idea whose hour has come'. This would lay upon Anglicans and their leaders a new and deep responsibility to be stewards of their historic witness, leading us forward with real humility to offer in the wider forum of all the Christian Churches the strength, checks and balances of our own tradition, while seeing also something of what that tradition has to offer in a climate of religious revival and renewal, which demands, as we have seen, careful and experienced shepherding if it is to avoid the pitfalls of many previous and similar renewal movements in our history.

So, it is first to history that we must turn. We need to rehearse, however briefly and inadequately, the story of Anglicanism and find within its evolution those very strands we have mentioned already as emerging unself-consciously throughout that story. For Anglicanism, unlike the great Churches of the Reformation, or even the Roman Catholic Church and similar to some extent to the Churches of the east, does not proceed from a systematic theology, or some great systematic theologian like Calvin or Thomas Aquinas. It is much more elusive than that. 'There is such a thing as Anglican theology and it is sorely needed at the present day. But because it is neither a system nor a confession . . . but a method, a use and a direction, it cannot be defined or even perceived as a "thing in itself", and it may elude the eyes of those who ask "What is it?" and "Where is it?" It has been proved, and will be proved again, by its fruits and its works.'[15]

It is to that evolving story of its fruits and its works (its history) that we must now turn our attention. We need to tell the story in flesh and blood terms before we seek to dissect the constituent elements of the theology latent within the story of Anglicanism.

34

NOTES

1. 2 Timothy 4.2
2. 1 John 5.8
3. Isaiah 42.5 ff.
4. viz. H. A. Williams, *True Resurrection*, Mitchell Beazley, 1972
5. St John 12.24
6. St John 16.21
7. Barbara Ward, *Only One Earth*, Penguin 1972, p. 297
8. A. M. Ramsey, *The Gospel and the Catholic Church*, Longmans, 1936, p. 220
9. Raynor C. Johnson, *Nurslings of Immortality*, Hodder & Stoughton Ltd, 1957, p. 149
10. *The Lambeth Conferences* [1867–1930], SPCK, 1948, p. 113 f.
11. C. Gore, *Roman Catholic Claims*, Murray, 1928, p. xii
12. F. Paget, *An Introduction to the Fifth Book of Hooker's Treatise of the Laws of Ecclesiastical Polity*, Clarendon Press, 1899, p. 226
13. Heber (ed.), *Works of Jeremy Taylor*, 1828, Vol. XI, p. 356
14. A. R. Vidler, *Essays in Liberality*, SCM Press, 1957, p. 166
15. A. M. Ramsey, *Theology*, Vol. XLVIII, SPCK, 1945, p. 2

3. The story of Anglicanism

THE EARLY YEARS

One must begin at the beginning where all good stories begin. The beginning is the beginning and not the divorce of Henry VIII and the endless saga of his wives! For too long, popular myth (perhaps not a little encouraged by critics of Anglicanism) has been all too ready to repeat the slogan that the Church of England was founded by Henry VIII. Not only is this a hopeless distortion of historical truth, but it is also attributing to that infamous king one thing which (in spite of all else), as a good Catholic layman with more than an unusually good grasp of Catholic theology, he would have repudiated most strongly. He was, after all, firmly made 'defender of the faith' and he knew that the faith which he defended certainly did not permit him to found a Church. The Anglican Church and Anglicanism is part of the universal, holy, catholic and apostolic Church and therefore can have no other founder than Christ himself and derives its charge and apostolic authority from the explosion of Pentecost and the apostolic command of Christ to go out and make disciples of all nations. There is no other possible beginning of the new beginning in history which we call the new covenant of the gospel of Jesus Christ.

1. Local and universal

But the wording of Christ's command is especially worth our attention, for it is matched in St Luke's account in Acts with a distinctive record of the nature of that first Pentecost. The command of Christ was universal in its application. There were to be no corners of the earth excluded. All nations were to be evangelized. But – and this again is a living and continuing tension right at the heart of Christianity – according to the record of Pentecost, 'they all heard in their own language' the record of the 'mighty works of God'.[1] The catholic, universal gospel of Jesus Christ is both universal *and* local. 'If it's real, it's local', as we say. So with the gospel. The worldwide, ageless ingredients of the good news must also find their expression in local form. There must be no dull, colourless, central totalitarian approach to this universal proclamation. Each nation and culture and each age will root the word in its own language, while also resisting the temptation to become eclectic and eccentric. 'Small is beautiful' is a dangerous half-truth, although in an age when, in so many ways, our world totters on the edges of totalitarianism, it is the other half of a two edged truth which we need to hear. Small and local is real and beautiful: large and universal is essential and unifying. Those are both halves of the same truth and in a real sense the Church of God has to hold on to both halves of that great truth if it is to fulfil the command of Christ. It is easy to see how through the ages the Church has lurched from one side of this double truth to the other. The rise of nationalism with its own language and the flowering of the vernacular is important, but if we err too far in the direction of national Churches we inevitably endorse fragmentation and disunity. The phrase 'the Church of England' or 'the Church of America' is in danger of such a fragmentation. We need something more like the Church *in* England or the Church *in* America. Of course this reassertion of the local, the vernacular and the national in a divisive sense is also a reaction against the wrong centralization and suppression of all that was local and indigenous. The Roman Catholic Church in the high middle ages and also from the Counter-Reformation onwards until recent times has tended to regiment and regularize every aspect of its life, its liturgy and its customs, and it is not surprising that both the Churches of the east and the Anglican Churches have protested in the name of what is local, flexible and distinctive. For in early centuries the Church at Rome accepted local emphases and local colourings, especially in the customs, canon law and liturgy of the Churches. It spoke quite happily of the Gallican Church or the Ambrosian rite and gave much freedom and varying expression to the worship and liturgy of the Churches holding together various rites (as they came to be called) within the unity of the spirit of the one universal catholic

Church. It was when such diversity was suppressed both in the Churches of the east and west that the local and, sadly, the nationalistic protests were soon voiced and voiced loudly.

It is not surprising therefore that we read of the *ecclesia anglicana* throughout the middle ages and long before the Reformation, denoting the sections of the one holy catholic Church found in the provinces of York and Canterbury. It was not seen in those days, and for many centuries, as divisive but rather as a proper diversification within unity. So the eastern Churches developed their doctrine and autocephalous (self-governing) provinces still within the framework and unity of catholicism until 1054. There can be no doubt that as we recover unity within the Churches some return to the earlier medieval pattern will be essential if we are to attain to the double-edged pattern of local *and* universal as expressions of the full catholicity of the universal gospel. (It ought to be said, furthermore, while in passing, that such a double-edged model is not just part of a system for ecclesiastical government, but is surely a model for which the whole world yearns and seeks as we necessarily become increasingly centralized as a global village, while rightly refusing any move in the direction of totalitarianism by cherishing, affirming and expressing what is local and what is national. Nationalism and totalitarianism are both ugly and dangerous distortions: a plague on both their houses. It is the responsibility of the Churches to seek some more excellent way and to offer this as good news and integral to the gospel, rather than to tackle the question solely as some mere ecclesiastical wrangling over models of church government.)

2. Ecclesia Anglicana and Augustine of Canterbury

So the concept of *ecclesia anglicana* is no Reformation or post-Reformation innovation. It is true that after the Reformation and in recent centuries, the title *ecclesia anglicana* or Anglicanism has developed. We now see it more in the terms of an emphasis, along the lines of the definition of Anglicanism as given in the *Oxford Dictionary of the Christian Church*.

Anglicanism 'properly applies to the system of doctrine and practice upheld by those Christians who are in religious communion with the See of Canterbury: it is especially used, in a somewhat more restricted sense, of that system in so far as it emphasizes its claims to possess a religious outlook distinguishable from that of other Christian communions, both Catholic and Protestant'. This was further expanded and defined by the statement from the Lambeth Conference of 1930 which outlined this emphasis in the following words: 'It is a fellowship within the one holy catholic and apostolic Church of those duly constituted dioceses, provinces or regional Churches in communion with the See of Canterbury which have the following characteristics in common – (a) They uphold and propagate the catholic and apostolic faith and order as they are generally set forth in the Book of Common Prayer as authorized in their several Churches. (b) They are particular or national Churches, and as such promote within each of their territories a national expression of Christian faith, life and worship. (c) They are bound together not by a central legislative and executive authority, but by mutual loyalty sustained through common council of the bishops in conference'. Put like that of course it can appear all too abstract. But in fact – in historical fact – it is not just an abstract idea like a breeze wafting in a more or less north westerly direction! On the contrary, like all Christian truths (as in the scriptures) it belongs to a people with a story to tell and that story is the living incarnation of that truth. The people and the story are primary; the emphasis or ethos is derivative and probably only becomes apparent at a later stage and in retrospect. Anglicanism is the story of a people first and foremost. As we progress, we will be able to discern particular features of emphases, recurring patterns and continuing protests against the tide of any external forces which tend to enforce either a more totalitarian church order, or seek to edit out variety, diversity and local outlook. In this struggle, the Pentecost principle of hearing and receiving the mighty works of God (and especially the worship of God) in our own tongue (the vernacular) will be especially significant at a particular turning point in the

Anglican story. So we are back again, necessarily to the beginning of a new beginning, with a story – the history of Anglicanism.

Although, as we shall see, this is not strictly beginning at the beginning, perhaps we could do no better than to make a start with the well known schoolboy story of Pope Gregory and the great Augustine walking in the streets of Rome and spotting two fair haired British slaves: *'Non angli sed angeli'*. Traditionally, we are led to believe that this issued in the mission of Augustine, the Benedictine monk, to the shores of England and to the site of Canterbury in the year AD 597. What did Augustine find when he arrived for his mission? Certainly we know that Bertha, the wife of King Ethelbert, was already a Christian and there is some evidence to suppose that the great Benedictine missionary monk and his colleagues would even have found in Kent some remaining fragments of British churches dating back to the times when Roman soldiers occupied Britain. The evidence is scanty, but sufficient for us to know that Augustine was not starting his mission from scratch. Such a British Church as Augustine found would have been of mongrel ancestry, as indeed by this time, and ever since, the British people have always been. Not much pedigree about this lot! It is true that according to a reference in Irenaeus, Britain was still unconverted in the last quarter of the second century (*c*. AD 175–200). Of course, wherever Roman soldiers were scattered and Roman trade routes extended, from Gaul to the tin mines of Cornwall or to the lead mines of the Mendips, there can be little doubt that even in that second century there would be some Christian presence. We do, however, know from Origen and Tertullian during the first quarter of the third century (AD 200–225) that Christianity had arrived (at least in the town areas) and had begun to spread. 'We may picture it as already deeply rooted in the populations of the shrunken and impoverished towns, and making its way by degrees among the peasantry. And . . . we may conjecture that it had already taken root over much of the highland zone.'[2] Certainly we know that by the year AD 314 the Church in Britain was strong enough to send three bishops (from London and possibly from York and Lincoln) to the Council of Arles as early as the very beginning of the fourth century and a further three bishops to the Council of Ariminum in AD 359. They appear to us as 'backwoods' men (and probably to their bishops at this council), for we happen to know that they were too poor to pay their own travelling expenses.

It was the political events of the middle of the fifth century with the invasion of the heathen Angles, Saxons and Jutes which broke up the presence of the British Church, which had formally and initially enjoyed some of the security of the Roman Empire and had even been pleased to build its early and simple churches on the very sites and under the protection of Roman garrisons. It was these churches in the towns which were driven away by invaders and the decay of many of the Roman centres of power in the aftermath of the Anglo-Saxon invaders. Through the missionary work of Illtyd (AD 450–535) in the mountains of Wales, Ninian (c. AD 360–432) and later, Patrick (c. AD 389–461), Christianity in Britain went west and then north to Scotland and to the life of the famous northern Celtic saints. St Columba founded the monastery on Iona (AD 563), and from Iona Aidan came in 634 to convert the northern English. The burst of Celtic Christianity relied no longer on the stable centres of civilization which had flourished in Rome and Britain, but as so often in times of insecurity and decay, its distinctive features were essentially in monastic communities which had flourished and become springs of living water in a desert of disintegration, anarchy and lawlessness. These holy men, like Columba, Aidan and, later, Cuthbert, were the craggy apostolic architects of an indigenous and earthy Christian faith and their power and authenticity still live on in that rugged environment of north-east England, Scotland and the extreme west in Ireland and Cornwall. 'To this day, their holiness infected the very stones and earth where they had toiled and prayed', so that Bede writing of this period will not disguise his sheer enthusiasm and delight at the irrepressible missionary zeal of St Cuthbert who 'was wont chiefly to resort to those places and preach in such villages, as being seated high up amid craggy uncouth mountains, were frightful to others to behold, and whose poverty and barbarity rendered them inaccessible to other teachers', often staying for 'a whole month before he returned home, continuing among the mountains to allure that rustic people by his preaching and example to heavenly employments'.

So, what indeed did Augustine find when he came to these shores at the close of the sixth century, and what was he to do with what he found? He found that he would be taking over, (if he were wise) where others, like Columba, who had died the very year of Augustine's arrival, left off. He found King Ethelbert's Queen Bertha with her chaplain whom she had brought to Kent from Gaul, worshipping in the little church of St Martin in Canterbury, rebuilt from a Roman ruin and situated only yards from the site of the great cathedral which Augustine and his monks were to build. In a word, he found a pretty rum lot! Nevertheless, he found an indigenous Christianity rooted in the soil which had survived many a blow and beating: a craggy and perhaps, by Roman and Italian cultural standards, an uncouth Christianity rooted in poverty and barbarity and still largely unweaned from a pagan environment, animistic, superstitious and strongly tinged with the habits and practices of the worship of heathen deities which stubbornly persisted only just beneath the surface of Christian missionary zeal. He found varying eucharistic rites which were different from those in Rome. If the evidence of the famous Book of Kells of the Celtic Church represents the local eucharistic habits of this period in the Irish Church, then we can still see in that beautifully designed book to this day, evidence of the flabellum, or fly-whisk, which was waved over the eucharistic elements in the Celtic Church as in some of the Eastern Orthodox Churches to this day. Yes, Augustine would find a colourful and variable, diverse ecclesiastical scene on arriving at Canterbury. What was he to do with this? Discount it, seek to obliterate it and start again? No. Happily he had received wise and catholic counsels from Pope Gregory the Great and perhaps even more happily, history has preserved for us the theological and evangelistic mandate which was given to Augustine at the outset of his task, from among the writings of Bede.

'The temples of the idols among that people,' wrote Pope Gregory to Augustine, by way of advice at the outset of his bewildering missionary task, 'should on no account be destroyed . . . It is a good idea to detach them from the service of the devil, and dedicate them to the service of the true God. And since they have a custom of sacrificing many oxen to demons, let some other solemnity be substituted . . . so that they may learn to slay their cattle in honour of God and for their own feasting . . . If they are allowed some worldly pleasures in this way, they are more likely to find their way to the true inner joys. For it is doubtless impossible to eradicate all errors at one stroke . . . just as the man who sets out to climb a high mountain does not advance by leaps and bounds, but goes upward step by step and pace by pace. It is in this way that the Lord revealed himself to the Israelite people.'[3] For Augustine was genuinely perplexed by what he found and not least in discovering a variety of liturgical forms and customs. 'Since we hold the same faith, why do customs vary in different churches, why does the method of saying Mass differ in the holy Roman Church and in the Churches of Gaul?'[4] To this practice of diversity and ecclesiastical pluralism, the reply of Gregory is prophetic and far reaching in its implications. Indeed it may not be too euphoric to see it as the very mandate to which a twentieth century ecumenical quest should turn for a model of multiplicity and diversity within unity.

And so Pope Gregory replies to Augustine: 'My brother, you are familiar with the usage of the Roman Church in which you were brought up. But if you have found customs, whether in the Church of Rome or of Gaul or of any other that may be more acceptable to God, I wish you to make a careful selection of them, and teach the Church of the English whatever you have been able to learn with profit from the various churches . . . For things should not be loved for the sake of places, but places for the sake of good things. Choose, therefore, from every Church those things that are pious, religious and upright, and when you have as it were made them up into one body, let the minds of the English be accustomed thereunto'.[5]

3. Struggles and tensions

So from the outset 'the Church of the English' was essentially a mixed bag by the time of Augustine at the close of the sixth century, and was not going to be subjected to a foreign import of a synthetic and alien diet, but was to be open to the opportunities offered from 'various churches' like a smorgasbord of differing and local diets. So much was this so, that a contemporary writer hazards that from the generous and genuinely catholic prescription handed by Pope Gregory to St Augustine we could see possibly here already 'the roots of the Anglican spirit of tolerance, reasonableness and comprehensiveness' even at this early date.[6] For it is interesting to note, as the same Roman Catholic author does, that 'not only St Augustine but also the four subsequent Archbishops of Canterbury, the first Archbishop of York, the first Bishop of London, the first Bishop of Rochester and the first Abbot of Canterbury Abbey (all saints) were all monks from the two groups sent by St Gregory from his Rome monastery; thus Gregory and his monks not only set up the basic diocesan structures that have continued up to the present in the Church of England, but also provided the pioneer churchmen who laid the human foundations for that Church'.[7] They were all out of the same stable and from the starting post gave the character and stamina to the race which subsequently has been the story of this Church of the English to our present day. For there were at least three if not four strands in Christianity of the early English Church: British, Celtic, Gallican and Roman. So Bishop Stephen Neill sees from the outset a tension within the fellowship of the English Church. 'Uniformity and variety, centralization and independence – there is a kind of ebb and flow in the life of the church between these poles. Much of the history of the English Church', he surmises, 'before the Reformation can be summed up in terms of the tension between these two ideals. Frequently it was the ecclesiastics who were in favour of uniformity, which in those times meant closer dependence on the See of Rome; whereas the monarchs on the whole were sturdy defenders of a measure of national independence.'[8]

This was the bone of contention at the famous Council of Whitby in 664. Such meat as there was, on this otherwise rather dry bone of ecclesiastical politics, was a concern for the fixing of the date of Easter. It so happens that the method of dating Easter has remained as one of the many expressions of what is local and variable in the life of the Church – especially in the Orthodox Churches of the east. There has always been a resistance to a centralization which demands uniformity of practice on secondary matters. For the Celtic Church the method of dating Easter represented such a local and indigenous practice and a similar resistance to the rigid uniformity being processed from Rome. It is interesting to notice that the Council or Synod at Whitby was convened and presided over by the local King – Oswy of Northumbria – and the Celtic case for the diversity of local practice, in the matter of dating Easter, was strongly pressed largely by the Celtic contingent and with the support of the king. However, the ability and eloquence of Wilfred of Ripon, speaking on behalf of the See of Peter, carried the day with a sentence and in presenting a case which, in its expression, is certainly worthy of note in our overall picture. He asked the synod, somewhat rhetorically, this question: 'Though your fathers were holy, do you think that their small number, in a corner of the remotest island, is to be preferred before the universal church of Christ throughout the world?' There is the issue in a proverbial nutshell. We may not want to say that what is small and local should be 'preferred before' the universal claims of the Catholic Church, but in secondary matters there should be room for local colouring and distinguishing diversity. However, the totalitarian case carried the day and on this occasion and with this king, the case for Rome and centralization won the argument and won the day.

There were to be other kings at other times and in different seasons who were to press more ruthlessly for the place of local

45

variation as indeed there were to be other clerics – largely Norman imports after 1066, William the Conqueror and all that – who were to press hard the continuing cry of Rome for uniformity, centralization and a streamlined, almost military, precision, bringing all into line and all into step. Archbishops of Canterbury from Lanfranc onwards (1005–1089) tended to be Pope's men, including surprisingly and by a kind of *volte face* the famous Thomas a Becket. Here again is a significant turning point in the Anglican story where the king won the battle but lost the day in the face of the unfortunate martyrdom of his great friend and papal advocate. The case for Roman centralization now had the blood of a martyr to strengthen its case and although subsequent kings took up the cause for more local jurisdiction and power of appointments, the arm of the papacy, strongly supported by European politics, proved stronger, not infrequently bringing kings and monarchs to heel and sometimes even to their knees.

THE ANGLICAN CHURCH AT THE REFORMATION

1. The Settlement of Henry VIII

However, there eventually arose a king who would win the argument, the battle and the day – Henry Tudor, Henry VIII. Of course, by this time, the environment of Europe was very different from that of the days of Henry II. There were many other forces, theological and religious as well as political and economic, which were battering on the medieval fortress of papal supremacy and demanding in the name of many and various causes a new relationship between the See of Peter and all other Christians in Europe. As long ago as 1054 the Churches of the East had broken away from an over demanding and highly western-orientated papacy, but now within Europe and in the west, other forces of fragmentation were at work, threatening further hostile divisions.

Space forbids any adequate analysis of the many and divisive forces at work in the sixteenth century Europe of the

Reformation era. We can do little more than list them here, but nevertheless underline each of them as a force of enormous and lasting importance in the developing and diversifying emphases which were subsequently to shatter the monochrome and institutionally united Church of the west. For it is these same emphases which need to be read carefully as all Christians five hundred years later seek to return to a unified Church which is not uniform and a Church which can contain in a single fellowship of the spirit the best of what is local and limited, as well as that which is universal and lasting.

It was Tyndale, in 1525, who had first translated the Bible into English, but by the beginning of the sixteenth century under the influence of the new learning of such men as Erasmus, the scholars of the Renaissance emphasized the need to return to the Greeks and the neoplatonist philosophies of the classical world. The Bible was becoming an open book with a gospel message in the language of the people. The invention of the printing press rapidly released across Europe a firsthand knowledge of the scriptures and brought in its wake a popular scriptural knowledge of the gospel with an accompanying scriptural piety which was soon to appear in sharp contrast with the late medieval Church of Rome. The new learning of the Renaissance, in the hands of sensitive and scholarly men of the calibre of Erasmus, Dean Colet of St Paul's and Thomas More, soon found itself also questioning the clericalism, the ignorance and a blatantly antiquarian authority in matters of doctrine and morals so brashly executed by the papacy. On both the grounds of scripture and the discipline of the new sciences, emerging in the Renaissance, men and women were vocalizing many questions which had grumbled away in earlier centuries, but which now erupted, and they refused alike to heed either the medieval weapon of excommunication or the power of the ecclesiastical courts to effect repression or punishment for the age-old cry of heresy.

So it is not surprising that the laity combined with the monarch and his or her appointed prelates to do battle with the papacy. The emerging consciousness of a strongly developed national monarchy throughout Europe was all too ready to give a sympathetic ear to the more radical reformers who were naturally and primarily concerned to work out theologies of a different church structure, and a more biblically-based spirituality, amplified and popularized by a new emphasis on the power and place of biblical preaching. The pulpit and the printing press were the new organs of this powerful and popular programme for reform which was sweeping throughout the whole of European civilization by the sixteenth century. Luther, Calvin and Zwingli headed the cast of a huge line of theological reformers, changing the map and face of Europe in the name of what history has agreed to call *the* Reformation. It was the convergence of these many and contemporary forces which finally shattered the totalitarian power of the papacy.

Yet, Henry VIII himself and his court, although they were all very much figures of the Renaissance and new learning were still nevertheless strongly Catholic. Henry was something of a theologian himself and persisted in raising many questions against the popular theological reforms which were gathering pace in Europe. It was not for nothing that the Pope had personally named Henry as 'Defender of the Faith' and Defender of the Faith he remained until his death. It is true that he wanted to be king in his own country, legally, politically and financially and furthermore that when he was faced with the divorce dilemma he refused to permit appeals to go over his head directly to the Pope unless the replies that came back from Rome were to his liking. Given the right balance of power in Europe at the time (always a tricky trio with France, England and Spain), there was no reason why the reply should not have been to his liking. However, the European balance of power was especially unbalanced from the point of view of the papacy at that precise moment in history and the decision therefore went against Henry. The battle had so many of the overtones of previous conflicts, but this time, the climate generally throughout Europe in politics, religion and economics conspired to give the edge of the argument to the king. Politically, legally and therefore in religious jurisdiction also, the realm of England separated from Rome. Nevertheless, Henry was not willing to take on board many of the other teachings of the continental reformers who were so eloquent throughout the Europe of his day. For example, in the Six Articles and the Ten Articles, the king reasserted the whole orchestration of Catholic practice and principles, and Cranmer, although wedded to both the vernacular and a wife, was constrained to limit his talents in the former to a translation of the litany into English and his exploits with the latter to the secret boundaries of his closet!

2. After Henry's death

During the brief reign of Henry's son, Edward VI (1547–53), the undiluted and persuasive forces of the continental Reformation were felt to the full in the English Church. Although the structures of the Church with its sacraments and the three-fold order of bishops, priests and deacons were retained (unlike the Churches of Geneva and most of the Protestant Churches of Europe) the flavour of English Christianity after the death of Henry VIII was increasingly and distinctively Calvinist, as Cranmer's years at Canterbury progressed between the first and second Prayer Books of 1549 and 1552. The preachers began to proclaim the pure Protestantism of Geneva from the English pulpits; many outward and visible signs of Catholic worship and order were abolished, forbidden or pushed out of the way in a wave of iconoclastic fervour, all to be reversed, however, under the reactionary queen of the Counter-Reformation – Mary Tudor (1553–58). For five years, after a general absolution to the nation proclaimed by Cardinal Pole from Parliament, for a while many (except those like Cranmer who died at the stake) were chorusing with a Vicar of Bray's flexibility a united chorus totally in favour of Rome, the Pope and a return to the Latin medieval practices of the previous centuries. It is very difficult indeed to assess how much, how extensive and how uniform this reactionary programme actually was practised by the Edwardian clergy and the people of the nation during those five years. Presumably, it was patchy and irregular and only a detailed and geographical survey would serve as an exact and fair picture – presuming such historical evidence is still available. What is quite certain, however, is that by the death of Mary Tudor in 1558, the new Queen Elizabeth was faced with an immediate and pressing need to unite Church and nation in a settlement which commanded religious acceptance and which was politically possible in the wider arena of European national politics. The fact that she did this during her long and distinctive reign from 1558 until 1603 is one of the real achievements of statemanship in history, demanding even then a fair share of luck and grace to succeed. It cost blood, as earlier actions and reactions had previously done, and there were many consciences which suffered from the compromising requirements of the new Elizabeth settlement. Yet seen in its historical perspective, it appears neither more repressive than Calvin's hold on Geneva nor more casuistical than Henry of Navarre in France who was later to declare, somewhat wearily, (though by no means unwisely) in 1593 that 'Paris was worth a Mass'. Twentieth century spectacles strongly tinted with the colouring of democracy are not especially helpful for viewing and reviewing the stormy events of the sixteenth and seventeenth century European political and religious settlements.

3. The Elizabethan way: Popery or Puritanism?

What emerges, however, either by grace, by accident or even by expediency in what we now know as the Elizabethan Settlement, with its prayer book of 1559, turned out in practice to be a remarkable confection of Christian belief and practice. The genius of this Elizabethan Settlement was its refusal to let go of the tension between popery and puritanism, by creating a 'middle way'. It was not, however, that kind of middle way which is no man's land, but rather that middle way which truly marks the point of intersection where two apparently conflicting viewpoints meet and perhaps, therefore, might more adequately be described as a crossroads rather than as a middle road. Two subsequent chapters of Anglican history were to let go of the tension and led the Anglican Church first into a reaction in the direction of popery and subsequently into the opposite direction of puritanism. Nevertheless it says much for the Elizabethan Settlement that what was established in the long reign of Elizabeth could weather later these comparatively short-lived (though often violent) storms.

Of course, much of this part of the story is political ('the art of the possible') and expedient. We must not expect in an incarnate faith like Christianity to find the jewels of gospel teaching with their accompanying theology and spirituality uncluttered by the foils of lesser motives and the accidents and sinful designs of human history. 'The truth', said Oscar Wilde, 'is rarely pure and never simple'.[9] It is all too easy for an assembled array of cynics, parading as supreme realists, to borrow from the more popular half-truths of economics, politics, sociology – to say nothing of psychology – and to make havoc of every chapter of history, reducing everything to the lowest common denominator and seeing only dirt, decay and deceit at every turn in the road. The whole history of God's revelation can be rewritten in that key if we are so determined. Misguidedly we can seek to salvage pure and spiritual activities with only pure and spiritual motives, but this is equally mistaken. It was said of the first reluctant king of Israel – King Saul – that he had 'hid himself among the stuff'.[10] So it was to be with the king of the new Israel. He did not appear bright and shining, antiseptic and clean on the pages of history. He also 'hid himself among the stuff' in an outhouse at the back of an inn in the back streets of Palestine. His birth is set in the grimy, political events of the city of Bethlehem, overshadowed – as it is to this day – by the large palace of King Herod with all that it meant. It was all in fact occasioned by a political census. His life and teaching were set, in fact, religiously and politically, within the unique combination of a vast and corrupt empire in tension with a vast and corrupt religious system in the period when Pilate was Procurator in Judea and when the decadent Herod was more influenced by than influencing a volatile community torn apart by religious factions at a particularly precarious moment in its history. Add to this the particular psychological weaknesses of his immediate friends and followers, the exploitation and decay of the Roman Empire to which we have referred above (preserving still the semblance of law and order together with the unique opportunities of travel and almost universal language), and we begin to see 'the stuff' of which revelation history is made. The Peace of Constantine, for example, in the year AD 313 was itself a piece of political expediency and yet it is into the very fibres of this kind of history that the revelation of God is woven. Of course it is possible to write all this story in such a way as to appear only pessimistic and to end with a superficial judgement of supreme cynicism in the words of the psalmist, 'Who will show us any good?'

Christian truth is always packaged in the stuff of historical events and the limitations of human personality. It does not take much effort to evaluate the former with purely secular motives and the latter, like power and absolute power as being merely corrupt, or even absolutely corrupt. Yet it is in our stories and the telling of them that we learn most about our inner selves and likewise it is in the events of history that we can – albeit only faintly – discern the hand of God at work.

For in fact the Elizabethan Settlement asserted some remarkable and – as history has shown – robust constituent elements in the establishing of a gospel Church and a Catholic Christianity. Yet Elizabeth in her diplomatic skills had to walk a tightrope throughout her long reign, refusing either to topple into the hands of the Puritans on the one hand or into the hands of the Papists on the other. So skilfully did she do this at the level of diplomacy and international politics, that the Pope waited over twenty years before finally excommunicating her. By this time, Elizabeth was secure and the spirit of England and Englishmen abroad was based upon loyalty – a loyalty which was to be essential for stability, internal peace and strong and confident foreign policy, not least towards Spain who delayed the Armada until 1588 (*after* the Bull of Excommunication). England was then strong enough in every way to rebuff such hostilities from without, and any divisions from within.

Behind all this diplomacy and political juggling, however, the theological basis for the continuing character of the Anglican Church was being established, with a theology and apologia largely written at the pen of one, Richard Hooker (1554–1600). Never violently anti-papist, yet stolidly opposed to Puritanism, in his principal work, *The Laws of Ecclesiastical Polity*, he drew together the traditions of the English Church in ways which gave to the Elizabethan Settlement a solid theological platform. Because of his doctrine of creation he was able to find a place for reason and experience within the tripartite model and method of doing his theology. Hooker constantly and forcefully asserted the importance of creation and its worth: 'All things that are, are good'. For Hooker, God is in all things, with the optimism of the opening verses of St John's Gospel, and although that image of God in his creation is marred, it is not totally eradicated. It was not therefore a long step from that assertion to see a place for reason in theology alongside the revelation of scripture and the traditions and teachings of the Church. The reason of man, of course, is clouded, but it is not destroyed. For Puritans, largely influenced by the Calvinist doctrine of total depravity and blowing strongly from the city of Geneva, such an optimistic view of human nature and the place of reason was not possible. Puritans were to rely solely upon scripture as interpreted by the Holy Spirit at work in individuals. For Hooker and for Anglicanism this position is too narrow and dangerously liable to confuse what Hooker dubbed as 'private fancies with the promptings of the Holy Spirit'. Puritans were prepared to give reason an authority in the realm of the sciences, but to limit it to that sphere, almost in a schizophrenic way, keeping theology in a separate compartment, unsoiled and untainted by anything so human as reason or human experience. In his teachings about prayer and spirituality the same spirit of optimism is apparent, because in an almost Pauline way he places a strong emphasis on the close and unique relationship between Christ and the Christian: that intimate indwelling which he sees as 'participation' – the same participation as exists at the very heart of the life of the blessed Trinity. So the great promise of St John's Gospel of the Father and the Son coming to abide and dwell in the heart of the faithful believer is taken at its word and much of Hooker's eucharistic devotion focuses upon this exact and particular doctrine. 'I in you and you in me' – strongly evocative of that distinctively Anglican prayer of humble access which requests with humility 'that we may ever more dwell in him and he in us.'* For Hooker, that is the whole basis of the inner life of the Christian, freeing that life from the self-conscious rigours and methods of prayer and placing all the emphasis on the inner yearnings of a relationship and friendship between Christ and the Christian, leaving Hooker to make the gorgeously optimistic yet telling affirmation: 'Everie good and holie desire, though it lacke the forme, hath notwithstandinge the force of a prayer'. Straight out of the same stable as Julian of Norwich, John Hilton and Richard Rolle and the English school of the fourteenth century, we hear in the writings of Hooker familiar themes re-orchestrated and presented to the mind and spirituality of the sixteenth century Elizabethan Settlement.

Furthermore, Hooker is adamant on the place for variety in what he calls 'the outward fashions' of church practice. 'Wilful singularity must be avoided, but so must rigid uniformity amongst churches'. In this and in so many ways, Hooker's teaching picked up the distinctive elements of the English Church prior to the Reformation and steered it through the dangerous cross-currents of Rome and Geneva in the sixteenth century, giving to subsequent history both theological principles and an eloquent mandate, more permanent and of more lasting significance than the historical, political and diplomatic constraints of Elizabeth's reign.

This balance was to be severely tested in the first half of the

---

*So strong is this emphasis that it leads to a distinction in eucharistic devotion which at its best steered Anglican practice away from the wrongly localized focus in the elements of the Eucharist. Hooker wrote: 'The real presence of Christ's most blessed body and blood, is not to be sought for in the sacrament but in the worthy receiver of the sacrament'.

next century, when under James I there appeared to be, to many of his critics, evidence of a swing back towards Rome. Murmurings from the Puritans in the reign of James I (1603–25) about his Romish tendencies, grew to a loud blast of opposition in the days of his successor, Charles I, and also in respect of the activities of his Archbishop of Canterbury, William Laud. The latter in matters of ceremonial, church furnishings and outward symbolism evoked great hostility from the Puritans, while the former, by his opposition to Parliament (a vocal Puritan stronghold) evoked equal if not greater hostility. The result for king and archbishop alike was the same: they were both beheaded, and under Cromwell for twelve years, England engaged in a Puritan experiment. Under Cromwell and the Commonwealth there appeared, once again to many others, to be equal evidence now of a swing towards the religion of Puritanism strongly flavoured with the teachings and influence of Calvin of Geneva. In retrospect, both of these movements proved to be the last of any such major political and religious turbulence, as the age of the restoration dawned with Charles II. The Act of Uniformity of 1660 and the reassertion of the Book of Common Prayer of the Elizabethan Settlement in most essentials in the famous year of 1662, restored the equilibrium of the Church of England.

What had emerged through the storms and tumults of the sixteenth and seventeenth century Reformation was a Church claiming an historical continuity both with that Church of the English of the days of Augustine of Canterbury, and also a catholicism bearing apostolic signs of the ancient orders and teachings of the early Church, but which had taken note of the spirit of reform with its new emphasis upon the place of scripture and worship in the vernacular, the place of the laity in the life of the Church. At the same time it appealed to reason and the deepest of mankind's validated experiences in the natural world, yet refused to lose the tension and dialectic of revelation through the scriptures and the traditions of the Church.

RENEWAL, CHANGE AND EXPANSION

1. Peace at all costs

Since the days of the Reformation the tensions have not
proved easy to live with, and in bringing our story up to date
we see 'the most spacious home and most elastic church in
Christendom', as Einar Molland calls the Anglican Church, as
a stormy and uncomfortable environment in which to grow
up. It never ceases to be a cause for amazement and dis-
approval to those outside the Church, that Christians can fight
so hard against each other. Christians must of course readily
acknowledge the sinfulness of divisions, but should never
believe that passionate concern for truth and justice will or
should evaporate into apathetic and balanced indifference.
Religious people feel strongly about their religion (hopefully
more strongly about it than about anything else) and therefore
the luxury or indulgence, as some would say, of a *laissez faire*
attitude is never a truly religious characteristic and should
never be extolled as a Christian virtue. The pain of religious
divisions is real and deep and cannot just be massaged away
with the therapy of loving words. What we must hope is that
each conviction strongly held will be transcended by a greater
truth and a more inspired insight and that we shall not be too
blind or too deaf to apprehend it when it is disclosed, until the
greatest truth of all – love – has really taken hold of us by the
scruff of the neck, finally hi-jacking us at last into heaven and
into the company of all the redeemed where knowledge and
peace walk hand-in-hand and where love and truth are but two
aspects of a single vision.

For the divisions in western Europe at the Reformation
period of over two hundred years had gone deep, shed much
blood, and scarred many people's lives, overturning the fortunes of monarchs and toppling the power of politics around a
single slogan or a careless theological nicety. All passions
spent, many, by the opening years of the eighteenth century,
were ready for peace at any price, and many Christians, not
least in the English Church, were by this time strongly

opposed to enthusiasm in religious matters in any shape or form. The age of enlightenment and the age of reason of Descartes, the French philosophers and the Georgian court of Handel, looked back at the ravages of the Reformation from the vantage point of Wren architecture rather as the latter twentieth century European looks back at the ravages of Nazi Germany and says quite adamantly: 'This must never happen again'. In any case, there was much in God's good world to explore, enjoy and evaluate, so that divisive religious issues were now to be placed further down the agenda in what we might well call, in twentieth century jargon, a lower profile. Latitudinarianism, as it was to be called, became the order of the day. An eighteenth century Georgian bishop would probably be diligent and caring in his pastorate, and still in the Anglican establishment hold much power and authority; he might even be quite a scholar but not so much now in philosophy as perhaps in the new sciences of anatomy, astronomy and mathematics, urbane, comprehensive in outlook and suspicious alike of extremes either towards Geneva on the one hand or Rome on the other. It was in this climate that the remarkable ministry and mission of John Wesley was born.

In many ways Wesley was a man ahead of his years (1703–91) and certainly born and ministering as an Anglican clergyman at a time when the broad church epoch of the Anglican story of the eighteenth century was not ready or able to hear him. As an Anglican clergyman he underwent a personal renewal and conversion of the heart, which left him unable any longer to be tamed or restrained by the cautious and latitudinarian Anglicanism of his day. In his Journal he tells us the moving story of that conversion which occurred on 24 May 1738. 'What occurred on Wednesday, 24, I think best to relate at large, after premising what may make it the better understood. Let him that cannot receive it ask of the Father of Lights, that he would give more light to him and me.

I think it was about five this morning that I opened my Testament on those words "There are given unto us exceeding great and precious promises, even that ye should be partakers of the divine nature." (2 Peter 1.4.) Just as I went out, I opened it again on those words, "Thou are not far from the kingdom of God". In the afternoon, I was asked to go to St Paul's. The anthem was, "Out of the deep have I called unto thee O Lord; Lord hear my voice. O let thine ears consider well the voice of my complaint. . ."

In the evening I went very willingly to a Society in Aldergate Street, where one was reading Luther's preface to the Epistle to the Romans. About a quarter before nine, while he was describing the change which God works in the heart through faith in Christ, I felt my heart strangely warmed. I felt I did trust in Christ, Christ alone for salvation. And an assurance was given to me, that he had taken away my sins, even mine, and saved me from the law of sin and death'.

The blunt truth is that the Anglican Church was not able to receive this nor indeed to receive the one whose experience it was. Yet in many ways it contained just the ingredients that the Anglican Church at its richest treasures most. It is worth noting the ingredients instrumental in Wesley's conversion experience – that 'warming of the heart'. Yet this experience is also set within the worship and structure of the Anglican Church in his visit to St Paul's Cathedral. It is not ashamed to borrow the insights of the continental Reformation in the person of Martin Luther in his famous preface to the Epistle to the Romans. It also contains that inner warming of the human heart and the human experience: the need to interiorize Christian truth and to make it our own with every aspect of our personality from the intellectual to the emotional, the inward religion of the heart and deepest experiences of mankind.

2. The challenge of renewal

That 'warming of the heart' soon became a consuming fire. So much so that what Wesley had to say was part of a real movement of the spirit and a profound prompting within the Church of England to renewal in the life of the spirit. Sadly at the time, however, the Church of England was not able to hear that summoning of the spirit and seemed deaf alike to the fuller claims of the gospel within the Church or to the beckoning call to go out to the new world outside – to America – for evangelism and missionary expansion. The Church of England – at least in general at this time – far from holding in tension the scriptures, tradition and reason, had lost that tension and tempered both Bible and Church with the sweet and apparent comprehensiveness of reason. Difficult tensions had been replaced by the ease of compromise in the name of comprehensiveness.

To such a Church, John Wesley constituted a radical recall to Bible Christianity and to evangelical experience. To Wren architecture and the somewhat bland and urbane environment of the day, however, such particularities seemed all too narrow-minded and intense. And so Methodism and all that it could have meant for renewal within the tripartite witness of Anglicanism was lost to the Church of England for nearly two centuries.

But with it there were other really serious losses also. The industrial revolution of the mid-eighteenth century was changing the face and shape of England. Massive movements of population from the country areas to the new large cities, especially in the midlands and the north, constituted huge deserts of poverty where the need for mission and evangelism rang out loud and clear. At the outset of the industrial revolution, the face and shape of the Church of England remained set and almost identical with what it had been since the middle ages when it had ministered to a largely rural society. Therefore, the new working classes, in the large new towns and cities of the industrial north of England at the outset of the industrial revolution failed in many areas to be evangelized by the established Church. It was precisely in these areas that Methodism was so effective: Methodism had proved to be flexible and ready to be out on the road and to preach and to teach wherever people were and not simply to be restricted to the established ecclesiastical centres of church buildings.

The second category which was largely untouched by the English Church in the eighteenth century was the category of the new learning. While it is true that many ecclesiastical figures were themselves pioneers and inventors in the new sciences, there was no real dialogue between the disciples of these new sciences and the Church at any serious or formative level. Often they were the same people – almost inevitably at this stage – yet the two disciplines went on in many areas in separate compartments of thought, preparing the way for the aggressive agnosticism of the nineteenth century, which soon prepared the way in its turn for a large percentage of English people to declare themselves as atheists or agnostics in the face of the new learning of the natural sciences. To both the social needs of the eighteenth century and the intellectual challenges of the sciences in the nineteenth century the established Church sadly appeared largely indifferent and almost totally deaf. By the close of the eighteenth century and the dawning of the nineteenth, both these forces of social need and intellectual inquiry had been welded together into a revolutionary weapon, most evident in the explosions and revolutions in France from 1789 onwards and the rash of revolutions which swept across Europe in the first half of the nineteenth century, reaching their climax in the revolutions of 1848. Revolution was in the air in England also and, as in France and Europe, it had directed its aggression against the monarchy and the establishment.

Little wonder that, in England, the Church, and not least the bishops of the Church, found themselves under severe attack. After all, one of the virtues of the Elizabethan Settlement had been to weld together into a single whole the Church and the nation, and by the nation it had meant the establishment and the monarchy. The monarchy, both Houses of Parliament, the bishops taking their seats in the Upper House, all alike now came under strong attack. The establishment of the Church of England was to feel the full force and blast of social and intellectual discontent as the years of Dickens and Darwin dawned. In 1833, the words of Thomas Arnold, the phlegmatic headmaster of Rugby, would almost certainly have been echoed by every sensitive Englishman of the day, when he wrote, 'The Church of England, as it now stands, no human power can save'.[11] In fact, with the benefit of historical hindsight, what he saw as the end turned out – as it so often does in Christian experience – to be a new beginning. For 1832–33 is generally regarded as the very year of religious reawakening within the Church of England and the beginning of a period of the largest missionary expansion of the Church since its earliest days.

3. Expansion and renewal

As the sociological and intellectual underpinnings which had accompanied the Elizabethan Settlement seemed to recede by the beginning of the nineteenth century, the Church of England was by this stage in serious need of deep and spiritual renewal.

It was therefore in some sense by the beginning of the nineteenth century that the Church of England was to return to its roots and to rediscover at a far more radical level than mere sociology and politics the very sap of its life. Those roots were, and are, as we have seen, the Bible, tradition and reason. The renewal in the nineteenth century of the Church of England is precisely a return to all three of these ingredients. Sadly it is often presented as a party issue, and all too easily we speak of the Oxford Movement and the Evangelical Revival. Much that occurred in the nineteenth century can easily be slotted into the party system of high church, low church or liberal but, frankly, that is a vast over-simplification. For the purposes of this Anglican story, which is hopefully above party divisions in the Church, let us apply the threefold model at least as the way of presenting this story.

When a group of Oxford dons began publishing 'Tracts for the Times', they were beginning a whole movement of renewal which has over the years rubbed off on the consciousness and practice of Anglicanism across all its membership. The occasion which fired off the subsequent firework display of doctrine was the famous Assize Sermon of 1833. In that sermon Keble challenged the Church to resite its foundations not on the 'sociological underpinnings' of the Elizabethan Settlement, but on the only foundations there really are for the catholic, apostolic Church of Jesus Christ – namely, Jesus Christ, the apostles and prophets being the chief cornerstone. The 'tracts for the times' which followed on from the challenge of that sermon and which were the doctrinal outworkings of all that Keble had said in his address to the judges became popularized as they were distributed throughout England. In short and terse pamphlet form, the tracts written by such scholars as Newman and Pusey, Keble and Froude, were intended to popularize traditions and teachings of the Church which went back to the apostles and which relied for its authority not on secular structures of the state and the establishment but which rather now broke through such superficial foundations – through the changing soils and quicksands of political national fortunes – deep down to the rock of a gospel Church, its traditions, its teachings and its sense of revelation. These tracts dealt with such matters as the nature of the Church, with a strong emphasis upon the apostolic succession and the consequent authority of the episcopate. Newman wrote one on the place of the Church of England as a *via media*, others on the place of Baptism and even one on the importance of fasting, but all alike strongly spiced with quotations from the writings of the early fathers. All these were 'marketed' largely to clergy throughout the country by some of the authors themselves riding around on horseback during the university vacations and distributing the tracts. In an age before the tape recorder (whatever did we do before tapes were invented?), this was the nearest to popular dissemination of Christian truth. Altogether, ninety such tracts were published in a few years and represented a massive resurgence of the doctrinal traditions of the Church of England. In those early days of the eighteen-thirties and eighteen-forties – the first generation of the Oxford Movement or Tractarian Movement, as it was sometimes appropriately called – there was little interest in ceremonial. The Oxford apostles were primarily interested in winning hearts and inflaming minds for Christ rather than multiplying garments. It was the lugubrious Dr Pusey – one of the principal Tractarians and a solid contributor to the tracts – who was once heard to remark: 'What is a cope?' This movement of renewal pointed the Church to the roots of theology and doctrine, the Bible and teaching: it was a theological renewal (of the kind needed again in the Church of our own day). It had the stamp of sound study and teaching, so that to this day when we are trying to place on the ecclesiastical spectrum a priest who teaches the 'full catholic faith without any of the trimmings' we tend to say that he is a good old-fashioned Tractarian. He is a good bird and sadly all too rare a species! It was only the second and third generation of the Oxford Movement who began to dress up and it is a sad or ironic comment that bishops and clergy of all kinds of persuasions today are all too ready to dress up, but fail so often to teach solidly and sturdily again and again, in season and out of season, the fullness of Catholic faith and tradition. In many ways we do not see the best side of this movement in what later came to be known – in rather party terms – as the Anglo-Catholic wing of the Church of England. So often it has tended to represent an unthinking attitude, largely based on a slavish copying of contemporary Roman Catholic practices and has failed in the one overriding characteristic which was and is its great insight – the communication of Christian faith and the content of Christian belief.

Parallel and almost exactly contemporary with the Oxford Movement was the Evangelical Revival originating from the other university of Cambridge and focussed on the remarkable figure of Charles Simeon. Here was an Evangelical who was evidently an Anglican and who owed his conversion to a careful preparation for the receiving of the sacrament of the Lord's Supper, which was expected of him once a term as a member of the university where the Anglican establishment of Elizabeth's reign still ruled, largely unquestioned. What Newman was to the Oxford Movement in the pulpit of St Mary's, Oxford, the University Church (for Tractarians were notable as preaching men of the pulpit as well as men of the altar), Simeon was to the pulpit of Holy Trinity, Cambridge. The infection of minds (that 'flame in the mind' again for which we pleaded earlier) is one of the continuing characteristics of the Christian record throughout the centuries. The debt that Augustine of Hippo (that other Augustine) owed to the preaching, teaching and proclamation of Ambrose in the fourth century, turned into a continuing and compounding credit down the centuries. Yet to each generation comes the challenge to produce some men who can reach the minds, hearts and wills and inner recesses of the human personality and redirect them into the ways of Christ and his catholic religion. Such a man was Charles Simeon, and again in that first generation of Evangelical renewal, emphasizing the second of our tripartite Anglican evidences, there was nothing of the later hardening into what came to be called the Low Church party – a resurgence of Calvinistic emphases. Indeed, so much was Simeon an Anglican that his critics used to say that he was more of a Prayer Book man than he was a Bible man. That was untrue and unfair, but it shows how rooted he was in the structures of Anglicanism, insisting that the witness of the scriptures and its outworkings in preaching and teaching are integral to a lively faith and an effective witness. As Newman was to topple over into the security of a more rigid Roman Catholic faith, and many of his disciples were to react into a hardened party position within the Church of England, so the disciples of Simeon were to become a party in the Church, fighting with their opposite numbers and toppling over into a Calvinistic religion, which the early generations of Anglicans had rejected, by steering a course in which the Bible and tradition could correct and inform each other. Both of these strands are necessary and it is interesting to see how renewal in either without the other leads to distortion and disunity. It was later Anglo-Catholics who tended to undervalue preaching, as it was later Evangelicals, and not Simeon and his contemporaries, who undervalued the Eucharist, the sacraments and the place of the Church in tradition and faith.

However, these two Anglican emphases still require the evidence of a third focus – the place of reason, and it is to the renewal of that ingredient in the nineteenth century that we now turn. The third renewal of the nineteenth century was the resurgence of the place of reason, and it focuses around the elusive figure of F. D. Maurice and the University of London – King's College. F. D. Maurice, maligned in his day, misunderstood by his ecclesiastical contemporaries and under-valued by later generations, heralded the return of a right dialogue between knowledge and faith. Faith and facts belong together. A faith without facts degenerates into superstition and finds itself continually on the defensive (arrogant and aggressive, for a defensive man is a frightened man and fear is not the basis of a living faith). Equally, fact without faith is, according to Kierkegaard, a prescription for lunacy which ends up by crippling the mind – and dividing the human spirit. The way of Augustine of Hippo is the royal road to intellectual and spiritual health – 'credo ut intelligam' – 'I believe in order that I may understand'. It is interesting to see how this movement, like the Oxford renewal and Evangelical renewal, starting as it did in the hands of Maurice, related strongly to the Bible and always acknowledged the place of a religion of revelation and not merely of rationalistic specula-tion. Nevertheless, by the end of the nineteenth century this movement had itself toppled over into the reductionism of rationalism and what later came to be known as the Modern Churchman's Movement, and a third party, opposed to the other two. So it was that liberal protestantism was born and championed.

Here we see, however, three parallel movements of renewal at work in nineteenth century Anglicanism, only later diverg-ing and dividing into parties as each loses touch with the other, or asserts primacy of one of the three parts. When either of the three becomes, in the words of Vidler, an 'exclu-sive system' then it leads to distortion, and – to use an old-fashioned word – heresy. Each of the three needs to take its place 'within the total orbit of Christian truth'. As we have seen, and shall see again, this leads to tension, but it is the tension of health and life, denying – as it must to any one ingredient – the cancerous assertion of totalitarianism.

4. Evangelism and Mission: the Church of Christ and the kingdom of God

Yet out of these renewals issued two or three important movements of which we need to take careful note. Missionary expansion, political and social concern, and the place of lay apologists were all three healthy and lively movements within Anglicanism by the close of the nineteenth century and beginning of the twentieth century. Looking back, it is hard to understand how Thomas Arnold could have been so wildly wrong in his calculations, unless one clings to the literalism of his pessimistic prognosis and simply retorts that of course 'no human power' can in any case, or at any time, 'save' the Church or, unless we see 1832 as the darkest moment before the dawn – that moment when, at last, *laus deo*, the Church, a nation, or person are finally brought to their knees. Such a moment of weakness is of course in reality supremely the moment of strength – that true strength which comes only as a gift to those who are empty enough and poor enough in spirit to receive it. The Church's breakdown was God's breakthrough.

In any case, the eighteen thirties were certainly a turning point. As the century continued, both Evangelicals and Tractarians began to reach out in missionary enterprise and the total of these endeavours represents one of the greatest missionary expansions in the whole history of the Church. The Society for the Propagation of the Gospel (founded 1701) and the Church Missionary Society (founded 1799) along with many other missionary societies flourished and developed in the nineteenth and twentieth century Church. Of course, like many, if not most missionary enterprises, it rested on the back of empire and used the facilities afforded by empire to pursue its ends. (Such had been the case of the first missionary expansion and its use of the facilities afforded by the Roman Empire of its day.) Furthermore with the advantage of hindsight, it is possible to criticize sharply the methods and message of these missionary agencies, who were all too ready to export the gospel and the English way of life as a single package and who were largely unattentive to the local and indigenous culture which they found in the course of their missionary journeys. Nevertheless, at this time, Anglicanism exploded beyond the bounds and limits of the Church of England and transcended the environment of its own history until by today the Anglican

Communion comprises twenty-seven provinces throughout the world.

The second outcrop of the renewal movements of the nineteenth century was a developing compassion for the new poor of the large industrial towns of the industrial revolution and a determination to bring the gospel from the sanctuary to the slums. While this sometimes represents only a narrow desire to win souls, and to leave the wider political, economic and social conditions unquestioned, such a judgement would be wildly inaccurate if it were accepted as representative of the complete picture. The early trade union movements, and political pressure groups like the Christian Social Union represent a real zeal for the kingdom of God and refreshingly pointed beyond the mere ecclesiastical concerns to the causes of justice, peace and the conditions of society at large. Whenever the full gospel has been preached, from the days of the reply of Jesus to John the Baptist and the missionary journeys of St Paul, 'the poor' have been the test of valid gospel concern, and certainly it is still the test of full gospel preaching to our own day. A gospel which does not point to the kingdom and enlist men and women in the combat and struggle and service of that kingdom, in all the particularities of political, economic and social concern, rapidly degenerates into an unhealthy pietism and a paralysed quietism. So, in the fifth century, St Chrysostom can write

'Would you honour the Body of Christ? Do not despise his nakedness; do not honour him here in Church clothed in silk vestments and then pass him by unclothed and frozen outside. Remember that he who said, "This is my Body", and made good his words, also said, "You saw me hungry and gave me no food", and "Insofar as you did it not to one of these, you did it not to me". In the first sense the body of Christ does not need clothing but worship from a pure heart. In the second sense it does need clothing and all the care we can give it. We must learn to be discerning Christians and to honour Christ in the way in which he wants to be honoured. I am not saying you should not give golden altar vessels and so on, but I am insisting that nothing can take the place of almsgiving. What is the use of loading Christ's table with golden cups while he himself is starving? Will you make a cup of gold, and withhold a cup of water? What use is it to adorn the altar with cloth of gold hangings and deny Christ a coat for his back? What would that profit you? Consider that Christ is that tramp who comes in need of a night's lodging. You turn him away and then start laying rugs on the floor, draping the walls, hanging lamps on silver chains from the columns. Adorn the house of God if you will, but do not forget your brother in distress; he is a temple of infinitely greater value'.[13]

The record of renewed Anglicanism in social concern and awareness is sufficiently conspicuous to contribute to a continuing challenge to each generation, while sadly falling far short of what the full gospel of Christ necessarily demands and refuses to allow us to forget. Both Catholic and Evangelical Anglicans have at their best witnessed to this ingredient of the gospel. Certainly, these nineteenth century renewal movements inspired men and women to work in areas to which their more latitudinarian forbears would never have gone. They founded nursing orders, schools and hospitals, and sent teachers, doctors and priests to many corners of the world. The inspiration and vision of these men and women was in fact nurtured in the establishment of nineteenth century Anglicanism. It was not all bad news!

The Clapham Sect was a group of Anglican Evangelical laymen at the beginning of the nineteenth century who took seriously the challenge of the social gospel and who, under the leadership of William Wilberforce (1759–1833), led the movement for the abolition of slavery. In a different key and from a rather different branch of Anglican nineteenth century renewal, W. G. Ward issued a similar challenge. In 1844 in his book, *Ideal of a Christian Church*, he wrote, 'A pure Church would with eager and urgent zeal have pleaded, clamoured, threatened on the workers' behalf. The Church *ought* to be the poor man's court of justice and her ordinary condition one of opposition to those in worldly status'.[14]

So, as the nineteenth century drew to a close, priests refreshed by these renewal movements, became visionaries and worked in the slums of the new large industrial cities, finding that their love of Christ motivated them most strongly in the love and care for his people and in every aspect of their lives. Housing, education and hospitals were high on their agenda. Frank Weston, the Anglican Bishop of Zanzibar (1908–24), in equally eloquent tones put the same challenge to pew-imprisoned Christians: 'Now go out into the highways and hedges, and look for Jesus in the ragged and naked, in the oppressed and sweated, in those who have lost hope, and in those who are struggling to make good. Look for Jesus in them; and when you find him, gird yourselves with his towel of fellowship and wash his feet in the person of your brethren'. Such was the power and extent of these various strands and streams of renewal which run through the history of Anglicanism in the nineteenth century.

The third outworking of these nineteenth century renewal movements within Anglicanism was the creation of a lay apostolate, who as international names, employed their skills as literary figures and turned them unashamedly to the purposes of theology and Christian apologetics. There was a whole galaxy of them. To list C. S. Lewis, T. S. Eliot, Dorothy L. Sayers, Charles Williams, is but to mention just a few Anglican lay people who really saw theology as the manifesting of lasting renewal and as the prerequisite of authentic evangelism. Just for a time, rather as in the Eastern Church for so long, the study of theology was not confined to the clergy, but was seen as the pursuit of the whole of the Church. Furthermore, in such movements as the Student Christian Movement, the cause of reason in faith was distinctively championed and the dialogue between faith and reason, science and religion eloquently taken up. Canon Charles Raven was distinctively an Anglican – almost an Anglican Teilhard de Chardin – and represented the very best of Anglican witness to the place of reason and knowledge in revelation and a right veneration for creation in some kind of natural theology. Such people lay themselves wide open to caricature and sometimes appear to more zealous spirits as even lacking in faith. Yet they are a vital and constituent element in the total witness to the total gospel, rooting God-talk in the world of matter and refusing to faith the wild delusions of grandeur or that citadel mentality in which it is protected from the challenge and questionings of thoughtful and sensitive men and women.

5. Anglicanism and the twentieth century

By the close of the nineteenth century and the beginning of the twentieth century, Anglicanism had torn itself free from the torpor of its eighteenth century latitudinarian *laissez-faire* and was more in tune for the conflicts and counterpoint of the twentieth century challenge. Where is it today? Does its three-fold witness to scripture, Church and reason stand today as a healthy prescription for further vitality with which to meet new opportunities for ecumenism on the one hand and the challenge of secularism on the other? Or, is it all too comprehensive and fudged at the edges, in an age which seems more ready (at least at the moment) to respond to apparently more authoritarian presentations of the gospel? Bishop William Wand wrote: 'On the evidence of friend and critic alike, the three most obvious features of Anglicanism are tolerance, restraint and learning. None of them is characteristic of mankind in the mass. Taken all together they may well prove a strange and unattractive climate for the man in the street'.[15]

Perhaps we should not give too much attention to such a warning. Yet, as congregations and membership of the Anglican Church in England and America have consistently and sharply decreased since the end of the Second World War, we need to do some homework, and to ask these and other searching questions about the place of Anglicanism in the worldwide supermarket of Christian options (to say nothing of other faiths) as we approach the end of the twentieth century. Let us forestall the last chapter of the Anglican story until we have done some more homework on our basic mandate in the following two chapters, and only then seek some kind of contemporary assessment of Anglican witness towards the end of the book.

NOTES

1. Acts 2.5 ff.
2. R. G. Collingwood and J. N. L. Myres, *Roman Britain and the English Settlements*, Oxford University Press, 2nd ed. 1937, p. 272
3. *Bede: A History of the English Church and People*, Book 1, Chapter 30, Penguin, 1968
4. Ibid. Chapter 27
5. Ibid.
6. Robert Hale, *Canterbury and Rome – Sister Churches*, Darton Longman & Todd, 1982, p. 85
7. Ibid. note 24, p. 100 f.
8. Stephen Neill, *Anglicanism*, Mowbray, 1977, p. 12
9. Oscar Wilde, *Lady Windermere's Fan*, 1891, Act I
10. 1 Samuel 10.22
11. Thomas Arnold, *Principles of Church Reform*, 1833
12. St Matthew 11.5
13. St John Chrysostom, *Homily 50*, 3–4
14. W. G. Ward, *Ideal of a Christian Church*, John Toovey, 1844, p. 31
15. J. W. C. Wand, *Anglicanism in History and Today*, Weidenfeld & Nicolson, 1961, p. 241

4. The Anglican model at work

We have been tracing the story of Anglicanism and trying to observe, albeit briefly and inadequately, selectively, and with somewhat erratic selectivity at that, the evolution of theological characteristics – the ways in which Anglicans talk about God and seek to discover his purposes and promises for them. Rather like the English political constitution, we have not been able to go to some document, or to the writings of some systematic theologian and pin-point these formulas of Anglicanism. This of course makes our task and the task of any interested inquirer more elusive, and sometimes frankly disappoints those who are looking for tidy structures and dogmatic exactitudes. Nevertheless, hopefully, what has evolved in Anglican witness has about it some consistency and character which bears the mark of a gospel Church, catholic in structure, liturgy and sacraments, sensitive to the insights of the Reformation, with its clear call to a biblically based faith and a personal knowledge and love of Jesus Christ as Saviour and Lord, yet also attentive to the reason and experience of mankind, even in those areas which would challenge the teaching of the Church or the record of scripture. As every deacon, priest and bishop has to say in the declaration of assent: 'The Church of England is part of the one, holy, catholic and apostolic church worshipping the one true God, Father, Son and Holy Spirit. It professes the faith uniquely revealed in the Holy Scriptures and set forth in the catholic creeds, which faith the Church is called upon to proclaim afresh in each generation. Led by the Holy Spirit, it has born witness to Christian truth in its historic formularies, the Thirty-nine Articles of Religion, the Book of Common Prayer and the ordering of Bishops, Priests and Deacons.' The newly ordained deacon or priest, or the newly instituted or licensed parish priest and vicar then has to signify his intention to be loyal to 'this inheritance of faith' and to use it as his 'inspiration and guidance under God in bringing the grace and truth of Christ to this generation and making him known to those' in his care.

As we see in these words there is a challenge that is contemporary, for the work of theology is ongoing and necessarily never complete in this world where we can only see the features of God and his purposes 'in a glass darkly'. So the deacon, priest or bishop, as a representative person – representing the whole people of God – is asked the direct question: 'Will you be loyal?' to an inheritance of faith (and tradition) yet at the same time refuse to see it as a deposit of faith locked in formulae and words of the past or even between the covers of the Bible, but rather as an 'inspiration' and as guidelines for bringing men and women in this generation to a living knowledge, and faith in, Jesus Christ. For 'with the changed cosmology, biology, psychology and anthropology of the twentieth century, a fresh theological approach to the formulation of the faith is inevitable'.[1]

How do we set about such a task? The answer is with real skill and knowledge of the tools of our trade, but never in isolation from the whole people of God and always setting our search and inquiry within the environment of worship, prayer and adoration. For, as Anthony Bloom reminds us so aptly, 'Theology is not knowing about God, even less is it knowing what other people have written about God. Theology is knowing God.' For to some extent, however inadequately and, of necessity, however humbly, the birthright of every baptized Christian lies in his or her claim to have 'the mind of Christ'[2] and also to 'have this mind' (or outlook or attitude) which is theirs 'in Christ Jesus'.[3]

Now that we have rehearsed the story of Anglicanism, we must relate that story to its constituent parts and see how each part acts as a check and balance to the others, creating an overall structure which can contain many varying insights and experiences, always rescuing them at the last moment from the disastrous tyranny of their own strengths and saving them from divisive disintegration. As we have seen, there will be three main evidences: the voice of the Church, its tradition, teaching and experience; the voice of the scriptures, and the voice of reason and human experience, the conscience and the still small voice. All three have a word, for they are all in some sense God's word to us – his revelation, mediated *through* the Church (not contained by the Church); mediated *through* scripture (yet not confined within the pages of the Bible); and mediated through the reasonable experience of mankind (though not limited to the rational processes of humankind). All three have a word because in some sense all were themselves the product of the word at work in creation and redemption. In each case it will be the work of the Holy Spirit, brooding over the waters on creation, overshadowing Mary at the conception, that word made flesh and eventually at work in and through the people of God in a Pentecostal outpouring. So it is that all three of these witnesses speak and testify to the one single and final word of God – Jesus Christ. In Anglican doctrine, each voice must be heard, for each is a word and a word we all need to hear if our gospel is to be full and our theology authentic. Furthermore each of these three evidences needs to be rescued from what will otherwise be a closed system. Each of them – the Bible, the tradition of the Church, and human reason and experience – can so easily become a closed system. It is the work of each of the three to penetrate, influence and infiltrate into the other. We can see in history recurring examples of how reason and experience, which at one time seemed to be so alien from the tradition and teaching of the Church, eventually succeeded in breaking into that tradition and teaching and a generation or so later became part of the received gospel and teaching of the Church.

In this way each system should help to correct and keep the other two open-ended. It is all too easy for one or other of these three evidences to play the tyrant: the tyranny of tradition; the tyranny of biblical literalism; the tyranny of rationalism. In the plenitude of Catholic Christianity each must interpenetrate the other if an environment of faith is to be created by the Holy Spirit and if the word made flesh is to be continuously incarnated in his body on earth – the Church – and in the life and experience of the people of God.

1. The evidence of reason and experience: the place of natural theology

It is important to start with this evidence, story or voice, because in one way it is where all theology must start – with creation. In a sense we have to ask ourselves some basic questions about the world of daily experience. Do I believe that it is essentially the responsible work of a creator or just the haphazard accident of a sequence of random events? If it is the latter, then, even supposing a God existed, the created world order would presumably tell us very little about him. Furthermore, the chances are that truth, and my apprehension of it, would be all in bits and pieces, unrelated and possibly unreliable because it was not consistent. Anglicanism contends that the above hypothesis and suggestion is not the truth. The Bible record is insistent that God the creator had, and has, a continuing and immediate hand in creating and that he has not yet finished this work of creation – that piece of handiwork which we call the world, creation or the cosmos. Furthermore, the Bible goes on to tell us that the spirit of God brooded over this creation. It goes further than this: it claims that the ultimate product at the peak of this created order was humankind bearing the image and the impress of the hand of the one who created it – namely God. Genesis choruses persistently and stubbornly: 'It was good' – God-like. It is true that, at the same time, scripture and even experience would suggest to us that creation is flawed and that the image of God in it is not perfect. Yet (unless we are Calvinists) we believe that something (however flawed) of the features and image of God is visible in God's creation and even in the summit of that creation – the fallen human race. For a large part of this argument, Anglican theology would appeal not only to the Bible but also to our experience as endorsed in such a view of creation. There is a highly convincing consistency of thought between philosophy, art, music and even the work of the scientist and physicist, and more than mere superficial research brings us to a moment of wonder and awe and suggests a shape and purpose and pattern in everything within us and around us. Of course many would claim with utter sincerity and integrity that such a conclusion eludes them and that *their* research in whatever quarter has not led them to such conclusions. Nevertheless, there is a strong and overriding consensus throughout many cultures and over many centuries which has never been able to come down on the side of atheism. Theism or deism has held the stage of human experience with most people most of the time in history.

Such is the departure point then in the thinking of Anglicanism. So, for Hooker, the cosmos was and is an unfolding of the mind of God in a structured and ordered hierarchy. All creation, although fallen and distorted by the sin of mankind, still participates to some degree in the mind of God – and this is visible, not least in the face of humankind. For the reason of God and the reason of man are not totally separate and contradictory. Whether we are looking down a microscope or through a telescope or listening to a stethoscope, the images we are wrestling with in some sense are related to the mind of God their creator. Such knowledge will not be *saving* knowledge (i.e. whole knowledge which can make us whole) but it will and does participate in God's own knowledge of us and has within it the 'seed' of that ultimate knowledge by which alone we can be saved. Of course, such a vision is lifted straight from Greek philosophy, whether Plato or Aristotle, and was consistently the view of all Christian theology for the first thousand years. Certainly in Eastern theology and conspicuously from the pen of Gregory of Nyssa (330–395) there was no hard and fast break between the evidence of the natural and the evidence of the supernatural. The continuity was not straightforward, and the one does not lead straight and simply into the other, yet they are *related* because they are the work of the one and the same Holy Spirit.

We find such a vision in all Catholic theology from Augustine of Hippo in the fourth century and early fifth century to Thomas Aquinas in the middle ages. Some would sometimes place more emphasis upon the continuity between the natural and the supernatural and some would place less. Some would place more emphasis upon the consequence of the fall and sin of mankind and some less; but all alike saw and witnessed *some* continuity of some kind and of some continuing image of God in creation and in man, however deformed or distorted.

However, it must be said that, in the theology of John Calvin of Geneva and also in his twentieth century counterpart – Karl Barth – a very different viewpoint has been championed. This is the view which is convinced that the fallen creation has broken this continuity irreparably and that the created order is totally depraved. Man's experience, even at its deepest, is deluded and his findings bear no relationship to the truth of God. Even worse, such findings will delude because they will masquerade as the truth and lead their disciples actually in the opposite direction from the mind and purposes of God. Only grace, conversion and redemption, such teaching would claim, opens to man the way to any saving knowledge of God.

Not unnaturally, such a viewpoint leads to a very different theology and a very different spirituality and ends up by making a very different sort of Christian. Of course it has the advantage of being streamlined in its appeal, definite in its propositions and powerful by its very distinctiveness and exclusiveness. It was this kind of theology which inspired the whole Puritan way of life at the Reformation and it was this kind of theology which Hooker consistently refuted from the pulpit of the Temple in the mornings while his Puritan adversary championed such Calvinistic theology from the same pulpit on Sunday afternoons! Yet that debate is still conspicuous in Christianity today.

Of course the Anglican position with its emphasis on the place of reason and human experience lays itself widely open to caricature and abuse. It is often known in the politics of the Church as the 'liberal position' and, taken to extremes, is always in danger of removing all the sting of the gospel and substituting mere common sense for that gospel; a rationalism where there should be a revelation: providence for progress; encouraging education to take the place of conversion and permitting the mind of mankind to replace the mind and judgement of God. Such a theology often tends to hold sway at times when all is going well in the world. It is at times when we are tempted to chorus, 'you've never had it so good' (as in the fifties), that liberal theology becomes most seductive in its wish to trim and tailor hard edges of Christianity and revelation so that they fit comfortably into our world view. It was precisely this kind of liberal Protestantism which Richard Niebuhr (born 1894) criticized in the following quotation:

'The romantic conception of the kingdom of God involved no discontinuities, no crises, no tragedies, or sacrifices, no loss of all things, no cross and resurrection. In ethics it reconciled the interests of the individual with those of society by means of faith in a natural identity of interests or in the benevolent, altruistic character of man. In politics and economics it slurred over national and class divisions, seeing only the growth of unity and ignoring the increase of self-assertion and exploitation. In religion it reconciled God and man by deifying the latter and humanizing the former . . . Christ the redeemer became Jesus the teacher or the spiritual genius in whom the religious capacities of mankind were fully developed . . . Evolution, growth, development, the culture of the religious life, the nurture of the kindly sentiments, the extension of humanitarian ideals, and the progress of civilization took the place of the Christian revolution . . .

A God without wrath brought men without sin into a kingdom without judgement through the ministrations of a Christ without a cross.'[4]

Yes, of course, liberalism with a capital 'L', once it runs amok, produces just this kind of soft edged Christianity that is in danger of having no cutting edge at all. But on the other hand, we have seen something in history of what happens to a theology, a Church and a Christian witness when no place is given in theology for the findings of human reason and experience. It leads to a fundamentalism either of the Church or the Bible, which looks at all knowledge *within* those sources and excommunicates or anathematizes every new discovery outside, from a Galileo to a Darwin and a Christopher Columbus to a Teilhard de Chardin. In the past it has frequently led to torture and inquisition in the middle ages and to the kind of torture and tensions of the mind experienced by Goss and many of the nineteenth century biologists, archaeologists and palaeontologists. It permits theology to topple in the direction of idolatry. For, once we refuse to admit that man is made and still sustained to some extent in the image of God, we promptly run off to make God in the image of man! The history of Christianity is cluttered with such bigotry and it does not make for wholesome reading. It belongs consistently to the history of extremism and fundamentalism. Anglicanism at its best has turned its back on such tidiness, however appealing, and has sought to include the liberal voice within the harmony of its chorus, while at the same time refusing it the place of a dominant and domineering soloist. The fatal result has occurred whenever a party of Liberalism occurred within the Anglican family. This is as much due to other parties and attitudes such as Catholic or Evangelical because they in turn have been most aggressive and extremist when the liberal position has been isolated and dominant. As in all good chorus work, each must be able to hear the other and to make appropriate responses and contributions.

For in Anglicanism at its best, the voice of the renaissance, of discovery, science and art and the still small voice of the inner stirrings of the human spirit have played a real part. This has been the basis of a strongly lay contribution to theology, ministry, witness and teaching, and it has also given real purpose and vision to a continuing concern for social justice, a concern for the poor and underprivileged and the steady refusal to prise apart the gospel from the so called social gospel. Its attitude to the evidence of all human experience at its deepest or highest, is neither to fall down and worship it nor to recoil from it and reject it. 'This is thou: neither is this thou.'[5] The evidence from creation and the natural order is always at best ambivalent. We shall find that we are engaging with conflicting evidences about the nature of God and the kind of God whom we are worshipping when we look at the evidence of nature and, furthermore, a nature which is red in tooth and claw: evidence about order and chaos or the unpredictable nature of matter and the cosmos. Our findings and our speculation must then be related to the other evidences of revelation and the witness of scripture and the Church. Only then shall we begin to have a living theology and especially a living theology which can relate to and resound with human suffering and the apparent cruelty of creation in everyday experience. Though we shall find much that leads to a cross in our experience and observations, we shall not discern *the* Cross there. Furthermore, we shall not find satisfying natural evidence of resurrection in all its fullness and all its irrefutable hope. At best, human reason and experience have led men to stoicism: at worst to hedonism, the pursuit of pleasure for its own sake, and the irresponsibility of the dictum – 'Let us eat and drink and be merry; for tomorrow we die'. Reason needs revelation; experience reaches out for that evangelizing which can only come through a knowledge of the saving events of Jesus in the Old and New Testaments and of being sustained in the fellowship and environment of worship, faith and service.

Nevertheless, at its best, Anglicanism has been a strong ally of the human quest. It is not insignificant that in the nineteenth century many parsons were local natural historians – entomologists, bird-watchers or butterfly collectors! The Anglican parson, often caricatured as being urbane, worldly or inconclusive in conviction and teaching, has nevertheless, at his best, taken his place *alongside* all other agencies for caring and for the building up of the community: ready to work alike together with the local society either for the preservation of the local village pond or the more chivalrous local committee set up for the care of single parent families. All this is no accident. It stems from a particular theological characteristic, which in turn takes seriously the story of human reason and human experience. Furthermore, such a conviction does not rest only on sentimental pantheism. For Christians it must surely rest on a conviction that creation is itself a word of God to us: 'God

80

spoke and said, "let there be light"; and there was light'. Light and enlightenment are a word of God, which even man's abuse has failed to silence totally. Yes, there is a word of God in his creation, and it is this conviction which not only permits Christians to acquire skills and disciplines which are worldly, but also *demands* that Christians will have a real love for the world (the created order), a right reverence for its beauty and order, and a responsible stewardship for all its resources. 'God so loved the world.' In that biblical statement it was the created cosmos (including mankind) which he loved, and which he loves. We must share in that love. We must respect it and act responsibly to it. The command in St John's Gospel to hate the world, derives from a different Greek word (aion) which means the passing age, the fads and fashions of a world-view which has turned its back on the creator. The true inspiration for responsible environmentalism, for example, should spring from such a love and concern. Indeed, we may want to go further and say that environmentalism, which itself is only a contemporary fad and fancy and which is not rooted in a truly godly view of creation, its value and its work, all too easily degenerates into a fetish, a new legalism, even almost a novel pharisaism, which is obsessed only with the outward 'cleaning of the cup'. Such, so often, is the character of an environmentalism which has not first heard that inner word which has finally broken through in the word made flesh and declared all things to be clean and pure potentially, when they are seen through the inner eye of those who are pure in heart. 'To the pure, all things are pure.'[6]

It should not be out of place here to refer to the work and witness of that good Anglican visionary, Canon Charles Raven, Regius Professor of Divinity in Cambridge, who died in 1964. In so many ways (not least even in his looks) he was an Anglican Teilhard de Chardin. Although his first discipline was theology, he was a keen scientist and especially well known as a keen ornithologist and botanist. In the frequently fierce debates between science and religion which were so characteristic of Cambridge University at the end of the nineteenth century and the first half of this century, Raven had a conspicuous and important place, refusing to be an advocate of either side in that debate as being over and against the other. To Raven, the world of religion and science was one: he deplored a wrong rivalry between the two when he wrote significantly in his book on Teilhard de Chardin, 'The theologians still discourse as if the music of the spheres or even of the fiddles had no necessary relationship with the instruments that transmit it, while the scientists in their professional capacity still insist . . . that the only explanation of a violin concerto must be in terms of the scraping of the tails of horses on the intestines of cats'.[7] In books entitled *The Creator Spirit* and *Evolution and the Christian Concept of God*, he reached forward for a unity of vision in his theology and science and so witnessed to a royal high road in his understanding and love of the universe which at best has always characterized Anglican theology.

For Christian vision at its best has never turned its back on the world but rather has found itself fascinated to the point where it is ready to see *through* the world. In the end there are only two alternatives: cynicism or contemplation. The cynic is disenchanted with the world and believes that all its promises are false. (Is it perhaps the disillusioned cynic who makes the best raw material either for puritanism or fundamentalism?) Christian perspective has seen through the world of matter, history and the frailty of humankind and yet at the same time has caught something of the glory of God made man the other side. It has seen the real place of the power of forgiveness over failure and in the end the permanence of God's love and grace by which we are enabled to say with Julian of Norwich, 'All will be well, all manner of things will be well'. In the end it may be little more than an echo of that earlier cry of confidence on the lips of St Paul: 'We know that in everything God works for good with those who love him'.[8]

So the evidence of reason and experience, often best heard in the courtroom, or the laboratory, in the operating theatre or the doctor's clinic, where ecclesiastical and clerical voices are seldom heard and never by right, is in the Christian perspective a word of God and when related to the word of God as the voice of the people of God, finds a rapport which also rings true – the harmony of a living and lively theology. Of course, as we have seen, the world has its 'fundamentalists' and those who are dogmatic and authoritarian in every branch of human learning. Scratch a 'liberal' and you will often find an uncompromising tyrant not far below the surface, who in the name of liberalism will demand the unquestioned worship of reason and human experience.

Historically, Protestants in the name of scripture, Catholics in the name of tradition and teaching of the Church, and Liberals in the name of reason and experience have all played the tyrant and had their little day. In reckoning the score there has been little to chose between them, except to apportion the blame fairly equally and to say that so often the tyranny and isolation of any one of our trio has been the principal cause of the over reaction of the others. It is in that threefold cord that real strength is to be found. For it is the strength of interdependences rather than of imperialism.

2. The Church's story – its tradition, teaching and evidence

Although they are set within history, drawing on the same sap of humanity, and still with feet of heavy clay, God has chosen a people in every generation to serve him and to be for him the focus of his purposes, his will and his power. Once again we are conscious of a voice and a word – a story to tell, even of a song to sing! The Church (whether we are thinking of the old Israel, the old covenant or the story of the new Israel, the new Covenant and the witness of the New Testament) is the *ecclesia* of God: that is, a people, chosen, called out to stand aside (not indifferently, but with humility and compassion) to cast another perspective upon the world. Such people have always been conscious that they were chosen: chosen not because of particular virtues and strengths, or for any obvious qualifications. On the contrary, they have often been the despised people of the world. Not many have been wise (according to the wisdom of the world), not many have had impressive qualifications of family title, background or social standing.[9] They have nearly always had more than their fair share (if there be such a thing) of 'undeserved' suffering. In some special sense they have been 'marked' men and women, called out (*ecclesia*) by God's word to them. They have had a life to live because they have first had a story to tell. They are the Israel of God.

At their best, it has been possible to see right through them! They have been emptied of self and filled with something given to them from God alone. Because they have not been *impressive* in their own right, they have been uniquely *expressive* of God's word in their lives as well as on their lips. They want to tell first and foremost what the Lord has done, before there is any talk of what they have done. Perhaps God can only choose people whose lives have been broken down and opened up to call on as vehicles of this kind of divine grace, as urgent messengers of his news and as silent witnesses to the eloquence of his word. They were frequently displaced people (aliens and square pegs in round holes) whose lives were seldom if ever straightforward. By standing at a tangent to the world, they brought a further perspective to that world, as bearers of a revealed insight. This holy people of God (and frequently and evidently not so holy!) were called and formed by God's word, that same word which informed the whole universe by its power, for the word which called out and chose the people of God is the same word who created the heavens and the earth. The teachings and traditions of the Church are not therefore the products of systematic theologians sitting down from time to time in history and releasing to the unsuspecting world a word from God. That word is mediated *through* the Church, that is to say *through* the lives of sinful men and women, called, justified and sanctified, but never acting like a medium and never impersonal. 'In many and various ways God spoke of old to our fathers by the prophets.'[10] So at the heart of this community of faith, almost in a Jungian sense, there is a collective subconscious knowledge of the word which brings to humanity's deepest experiences the sense of *déja vu*. For this revealed word must necessarily take on the form of different cultures, different faces and vocabularies, like a recurring Pentecost, in which again and again throughout history men and women are continually witnessing *in their own language* to the mighty works of God. So the revealed word in the tradition and teaching of the Church must not be set over and against the 'contaminated' word which comes through reason and human experience.

It brings a bifocal depth to reality, correcting and sometimes apparently contradicting the flat and single perspective of worldly wisdom but, at its best, giving it a depth and colouring which is inspiring to the beholder who in frequent tones will often be heard to exclaim – 'Oh, now I see'.

What sort of authority is this and where do we find its expressions? As we have seen previously, the voice of this authority in Anglicanism is often elusive. Anglicanism has preferred in the first place less definition rather than more definition and has restricted to a minimum, rather than extended to a maximum, the absolutely essential doctrines – that is, essential to salvation – or saving knowledge. It has preferred to restrict this body of doctrine and to rest it upon the creeds, the first four universal Councils of the Church and the consensus of the faithful throughout the ages. So the 1938 report on Anglican doctrine writes, 'The faith and doctrine of Christianity are handed down to us in the context of a living fellowship'.[11] That fellowship is primarily the fellowship of the Holy Spirit who forms the word of God in the flesh and blood of human history and the life of the Church, as surely as he formed the word in the flesh and blood of the womb of the Virgin Mary. So in some real sense – more than merely metaphorical – the Church, again by the action of that same Holy Spirit, is the body of Christ and its teaching bears the authority of Christ who has promised to be with it to the end of the ages and to lead it into all truth. The dangers of this approach are of course obvious and manifold.

In the first place, we might well ask how dynamic the doctrine and teaching of the Church can be with this kind of model? Is it tied in a rather static way, to the creeds and the teaching of the Councils of the undivided Church? Hopefully not. Like all life there must be room for development and even change; for 'to live is to change and to be perfect is to have changed often'.[12] How can we assess true change from false change: proper development from improper development? We shall be looking at these questions in more detail later in the book, but suffice it to say, at this point, that Anglicanism has cherished the voice of the whole fellowship of the Church and not merely its clerical voice or even solely the voice of the episcopate. So, 'this authority, in so far as it is derived from such a *consensus fidelium*, rests upon the range and quality of the manifold experience which that consensus gathers up, and upon the witness which, alike in the devotional and other practice of Christians generally, and in the doctrine of the theologians, it bears to the truth of the gospel. The weight of the *consensus fidelium* does not depend on mere numbers, or on the extension of a belief at any one time, but on continuance through the ages and the extent to which the consensus is genuinely free'.[13]

It itself, that approach is not intended to champion democracy, but rather to live out in practice the promise and power of Pentecost given to *all* the faithful and not to draw a false line between the apostolate of the bishops and the apostolate of the whole people of God. Such an approach inevitably leads to conflict and it can well be asked, as we shall see later, how and in what ways the voice of the synods of the Church today really reflect the *consensus fidelium*. What is the place and power of such a meeting as the meeting of the Anglican Bishops at Lambeth? Where there is conflict, who has the last say? And, is there a person and a place to whom Christians (not well versed in the history of Christian doctrine) may turn for guidance and teaching?

What is important to establish at this point, however, is the place of the tradition, teaching and voice of the Church in relation to reason and scripture. So, says the Doctrine Commission: 'The authority of the Church in the realm of doctrine arises from its commission to preach the gospel to all the world, and the promises, accompanying that commission, that the Lord would always be with his disciples, and that the

Holy Spirit would lead them into all the truth'.[14] The Church is a divinely chosen perspective *through* which we discern the essential features of God, but seen by Anglicans as only one of three perspectives and not in isolation from the evidence of reason and the evidence of the scriptures.

Whenever the Church has claimed isolated, unchecked authority (especially in chapters of its history when this has coincided with its possession of temporal power) it has been arrogant and corrupt. It has excommunicated new thinking sometimes for little better reasoning than that it is new and different from the old. So it was the great churchman Faber who could write (Roman Catholic though he became) the essentially Anglican words:

> For the love of God is broader
> Then the measures of man's mind;
> And the heart of the Eternal
> Is most wonderfully kind.
> But we make his love too narrow
> By false limits of our own;
> And we magnify his strictness
> With a zeal he will not own.

Equally dangerous are those in the Church who would place the teaching of the Church *above* the record of scripture. So Bishop Michael Ramsey rightly reminds us: 'The bona fide Anglican can never suffer the Latin scholastics to dominate the theology of the Church. This refusal need not involve a deprecation of what the scholastics can do in the field of Christian philosophy. But the refusal must be made, because the scholastic would substitute other categories than those of the Bible at the very heart of theology, where the Anglican believes that only the Bible categories can rule'.[15] Whenever the dogma of the Church has lost its rapport with the word of scripture it has degenerated into concepts and ideas, unruffled by the immediacy which alone is derived from the sense of the word of God essentially focused in a person – even Jesus

Christ, the word made flesh. Such isolation of dogma leads inevitably to casuistry. Of course such fundamentalism – for that is what it is, with all the appeal that fundamentalism can make in an age of instability and fear – is neat and tidy, easy to promulgate and not difficult to swallow to certain temperaments at certain points in their history. It is perhaps the only next step that is possible for them in their long pilgrimage, but it is sadly a long way from the scriptural understanding of the nature of faith as essentially involving all the hazards of a long journey through unknown territory. It was Malcolm Muggeridge, the tired intellectual gadfly of the seventies who, at the age of the seventy-nine, sank into the arms of the Roman Catholic Church with these rather weary, astonishing and sad words: 'It is rather like when you fall in love with a woman and ask her to marry you. You know there are no more questions to be asked'.[16] A strange understanding of faith and possibly an even more disastrous doctrine of matrimony! Surely if New Testament discipleship is anything to go by, that is when all the questions begin!

In popular thought, the Church is a ship (not a harbour or even a lighthouse) and ships are not protected from the storms and waves around them. On the contrary, the storms are felt most acutely by those who, as explorers and adventurers, seek to sail the seas and not just romanticize them, write poetry about them or even paint or draw them in the security of the landlubber! Far from being promised an easy crossing, the experience of the Church throughout its history has certainly not been one of peace, calm and quiet, or an indifference to the storms of the world. It is true that we have been promised that it will not ever ultimately sink, though that is poor comfort to those suffering seasickness, who might well prefer the end of everything to continuous upheavals within and without!

Yet, of course, there must be a real sense in which the teaching of the Church is clear and resolute, ready to address itself to each new generation with a contemporary clarity, seeking to express the timeless mind and purposes of God as revealed in Jesus Christ. It will do this best when it is most concerned with the kingdom of God and rather less concerned with mere ecclesiastical cosmetics, and when it points *beyond* itself to the God in whose kingdom the Church will find its true and appropriate place. When it is pointing mankind to the kingdom and beyond selfconscious ecclesiasticism, it will find itself rubbing shoulders with all kinds of men and women of goodwill who may not necessarily share the commitment of the Church to the particularities of the person of Jesus Christ and his revealing word. Far from this being disturbing, it should be encouraging and should help to bring about a genuine openness to the light of reason and human experience to which we have referred earlier. For as Michael Ramsey says of the early Church: 'The mistake of ecclesiasticism through the ages has been to believe in the Church as a kind of thing-in-itself. The apostles never regarded the Church as a thing-in-itself. Their faith was in God, who raised Jesus from the dead, and they knew the power of his resurrection to be at work in them and in their fellow believers despite the unworthiness of them all. That is always the nature of true belief in the Church. It is a laying hold on the power of the resurrection'.[17] Such obedience to the kingdom and such unselfconsciousness in the pursuit of truth will enable us to authenticate Christianity by believing that if Christianity is true, it is true not because it is Christianity but because in the end it is true.

Of course, the experience of the Church over the centuries and the presence of the Holy Spirit as a gift at work through its members, should give to inexperienced travellers valuable guidance and strong, articulate encouragement: the encouragement and guidance to which we rightly look in an experienced guide when we are trying our legs on the lower slopes in mountaineering, whose skill and accumulated knowledge and experience are invaluable and even ignored at our peril. The attitude of 'Everyone is out of step except our Johnnie', does not make for long life as a mountaineer and does not generally lead to that fullness and quality of life which the Bible calls abundant or eternal life. The Church really does have something to say on many issues and there is a real responsibility to its ordinary disciples who read the *Daily Mirror* or their equivalent in every generation. Those to whom the particular responsibility to teach and communicate the gospel and all its ramifications has been given should lay hold of this responsibility with a real sense of love and awe as a man takes hold of his wife according to the Prayer Book of 1662, 'discreetly, soberly and in the fear of God', not 'unadvisedly, lightly or wantonly'! The responsibility to hand on to others what we ourselves have first received and made our own – in other words our tradition – is a real stewardship and a terrifying responsibility. 'The Church has a right to satisfy itself that those who teach in its name adequately represent and express its mind.'[18]

Perhaps the first responsibility is the willingness by teachers in the Church to keep on saying the same things again and again. That does not have to be dull. On the contrary it should stretch the imagination at every point. Nevertheless it should avoid the spectacular or the sense of innovation for its own sake in what Christopher Booker has called 'the cult of the neophiliacs'.[19] There are occasions when St Paul, for example, deliberately contrasts his own opinion of a matter with other occasions where he believes that his message is part of the tradition received from the Lord himself. Any teacher of the Christian tradition (and especially bishops) should be especially mindful of that distinction and be ready to use it with humility and humour.

For of course, every generation needs to hear the same old story, but in possibly new language and with fresh insights: 'Tell me the old, old story'. Nevertheless, such faithfulness to tradition need not chain the Church to past statements and make them into infallible end-products. They are like signposts – departure points for further exploration. The Thirty-Nine Articles, in their historical setting, were precious as marking out the Anglican way, not against a neutral background, but rather against a background in which there was already a loading and a tendency in various directions. They are still precious to this day, but the background is different in its loading in the twentieth century and the same Anglican way will not be best articulated by a fundamentalist approach to the exact wording of these formularies. The letter will kill; only the spirit will give life and sustain that life in the very different world of the twentieth century and in the ecclesiastical climate of our own day. 'Unless one changes one cannot even remain the same: yet the change must remain continuous with what went before.'[20]

So the continuing responsibility and precious task of theology and theologians in each generation, is a holy and important task. But it is a task which should not be conditioned by the claustrophobic environment of intellectualism nor does it thrive best in the stuffy atmosphere of lecture rooms, libraries and common rooms. Theology is the property of the whole Church and thrives best in the environment of worship, prayer and the everyday Christian life of believers. There it can be tested, rescued from obscurity and mere intellectual niceties and clothed in outward forms appropriate for the abrasive encounters of everyday life where men and women wrestle in an everyday world with the life of faith. *Lex orandi* and *lex credendi* belong together. The Christian must test what he believes about God in the ways in which he worships and, vice versa, all this must be tested and proved by the way he lives and with those whom he loves and trusts. Belief, belonging and behaviour are inseparable and represent the fullness of the Christian tradition in the theology and teaching of the Church. Orthodox traditional teaching by the Church should commend itself by its catholic wholeness. Put another way, what Christians believe should fashion what sort of people Christians are. In a word, it should make saints.

Saints (holy men and women) are in their turn the best advertisement for and commendation of the teaching and faith of the Church. The more saints in every generation enflesh the message of the gospel, the less books will be needed to defend and propagate that message as being orthodox. Anglicanism, with typical flexibility, does not have a cut and dried system with all the legalities of the Roman Church for categorizing and eventually canonizing saints. It is perhaps typical of the Roman Catholic tradition, with its eye for precision and its history of legalism, that it should bring even to this part of the discussion such precise criteria for the recognition of that most elusive of all characteristics – sanctity. Nevertheless, it has to be said that a Church which does not sense the need to prove and test its teaching in the sanctity of the lives of those who are its members, has failed to see the vital connection between belief and behaviour, and the way in which that belief is given a fresh face, always recognizable, in each and every generation. The tradition and teaching of the Church has gone awry in an age or in any part of the Church where there is a conspicuous dearth of sanctity.

3. The record of the scriptures and the evidence of the Bible

It is no accident that the Bible has a special place in the record of Anglicanism and that its language and message are so clearly stamped upon the spirituality and public worship of the Anglican Church. Bishop William Wand writes: 'Merely as a matter of fact, . . . Anglicans . . . in their public worship use the Bible more than any other body of Christians'. He goes on: 'This does not, unfortunately, apply to private use in the home, where in modern times members of the Free Churches have probably passed the standard set by the average Anglican. But as far as public worship is concerned there can be no doubt. Anglicans do read the Bible in church more than other Christians'.[21] From the outset it may be necessary to acknowledge an historical rider to that comment by Bishop Wand, which was written in 1961, before the effects of Vatican II upon the liturgy and worship and spirituality of the Roman Catholic Church. It is probably true to say today, that that Church in its renewal vies very strongly with Anglicanism in its scriptural emphasis and in the bulk of scriptural content in its liturgy, for its renewal was very much a renewal issuing out of a new emphasis upon the place of the scriptures in the life of the Church.

However, Anglicanism at the Reformation had experienced this renewal in the sixteenth century when both printing and the vernacular translations exploded the Christian mind of western Christendom bringing new and rugged demands for a scriptural sensitivity. Necessarily, for the first one and a half thousand years of its life, the New Testament (and by implication the Old Testament as well) was largely a closed book to most ordinary members of the Christian Church. Copies, before the days of printing, were not easy to come by, except to scholars and monastic communities, while the barriers of language and literacy restricted the reading of the Bible to a small minority of Christians. In the west, the reading of the scriptures at the liturgy would be in Latin. All these circumstances in themselves conspired to give to the pre-Reformation Church an imbalance in its diet of word and sacrament. It was, almost inevitably, the visible action of the Mass, with its mystery all too readily giving way to superstition, which was the distinctive character of western Catholic spirituality up to the middle ages. It is hard to say whether the clericalism of the middle ages was the result or cause of this situation, but there can be little disagreement about the effects and outcome. The priest saying the Mass and the people hearing Mass was the staple diet of western Catholicism until the Renaissance and the Reformation. The practice and spirituality of these centuries went practically unchecked – at least in the popular piety of the day – by the word of God as read, proclaimed or preached from scripture.

The breakthrough of the Reformation and indeed the foundation of many of the Reformation Churches represented a strong and even violent reaction against the medieval situation. The Mass without preaching or biblical spirituality was replaced by the Bible and a new priority for preaching, in its turn suppressing the Mass and leading to a serious deficiency in the place of a truly sacramental spirituality. In the place of the cult and the superstition of the Mass, the Reformation erected a new idol – the protestant cult and superstition of the Bible. The new printing presses and a multitude of translations into the vernacular opened a book which had been largely closed for centuries. Henry VIII found it necessary to chain the great Bible to the lectern, not so much to enable every Tom, Dick and Harry to read it (because most people still could not read it even in its new translation) but rather to prevent it from becoming, in a wrong sense, the property of the populace. It is difficult for the modern mind to realize the inflammatory power attached to words, to a book and to preaching and the opening of the word of God to the people of God. The words of this book literally entered the psyche of the whole of the western world, disturbing and releasing strange powers latent within the Christian imagination for many centuries. The writings and drawings of Blake, perhaps more than anything else show something of the strange power of scripture – as strange and as cultic as anything associated with the medieval cult of the Mass.

So, it was not long before the idolatry of the Mass associated with the medieval world was replaced by a new idolatry – the idolatry of the Bible. 'The new presbyter is but old priest writ large' and *mutatis mutandis* – the cult of the Bible was but the old medieval Mass-cult writ large and the power of the preacher in the pulpit ('six feet above contradiction') was but the old power of the Mass priest writ large. One distortion was replaced by another: pulpits were in; altars were out: murals and statues were out and Bibles were in.

Once again, however, Anglicanism in its official formularies succeeded in striking something of a balance which, without wishing to sound smug, has given to Anglicanism a poise and inner resistance frequently envied by other Churches. It went back in fact to the 'classic statement of patristic teaching', the *Commonitorium* of Vincent of Lerinum (*c*. AD 450) where it was stated that 'scripture is sufficient and more than sufficient' though its right interpretation is to be found by reference to the 'agreement of the whole Church in all times and places' – 'what has been believed everywhere, always and by all'. In other words, the Bible in Anglicanism takes up its right place *within* the life of the worshipping and believing community. Word and sacrament belong together, as the balanced diet of God's people and the tradition and teaching of the Church and the teaching of the scriptures constitute a dialogue at the very heart of Christian faith and practice. The medieval and Reformation war of word *versus* sacrament, and Bible *versus* Church, enters into a treaty of mutual respect and a single synthesis of authority. In Anglicanism, the word and sacrament belong together and refuse to be divorced, even on the grounds of medieval desertion of the one from the other over many centuries. Furthermore, such a marriage is essentially a partnership in which neither partner is permitted the role of dictator or can claim an ultimate authority. When the Church is tempted to play fast and loose, article 6 and article 20 from the Thirty-nine Articles are eloquent in their rebuke: 'Holy Scripture containeth all things necessary to salvation: so that whatsoever is not read therein, nor may be proved thereby, is not to be required of any man, that it should be believed as an article of the Faith, or be thought requisite and necessary to salvation' (Article 6). And again, 'It is not lawful for the Church to ordain anything that is contrary to God's Word written, neither may it so expound one place of Scripture, that it be repugnant to another'. The dialogue is reaffirmed in the next sentence of Article 20: 'Wherefore, although the Church be a witness and a keeper of holy Writ yet, as it ought not to decree anything against the same, so besides the same ought it not to enforce anything to be believed for necessity of Salvation'.

This is no middle course for its own sake, but belongs to a tradition and theology of the relationship between the Bible and Church, which was reaffirmed by Anglicanism at the Reformation and which we now need to examine briefly as we seek to understand the right place of the evidence of the scriptures in the complex of experience and doctrine within Anglicanism. 'It would be wrong', writes Bishop Michael Ramsey, 'to infer from the exalted place of the Bible in every form of Christianity that Christianity is the religion of a Book. The central fact of Christianity is not a Book but a Person – Jesus Christ, himself described as the Word of God.'[22] That is the nub of the issue. The law and the prophets in the old Israel, and the life, sacraments and liturgy of the Church in the new Israel, both alike point to Jesus, the word made flesh. Furthermore, both the law and the prophets in the old Israel and the life, sacraments and liturgy of the Church in the new Israel existed primarily as an experience and in an oral tradition, *before* they were written down. In both cases – the old and the new Israel alike – experience and activity preceded any written word and the written word belongs in the deepest sense to that new experience and tradition. 'Under both the old Covenant and the new, the Church preceded the Bible.'[23] It was within Israel, with its prophets and priests, its oral traditions and its cults that the Old Testament was made. It was within the new Israel, with its apostles and prophets, its sacraments and oral traditions that the New Testament was made. So the conclusion is self-evident: 'within the Church of God, word and sacrament interpret one another'[24] and the focus of that interpretation is both before and beyond either the Church or the Bible – namely the word of God, Jesus the Christ. Neither the Church nor the Bible are ends in themselves – they both point beyond themselves to the one who is before, within and beyond them all – Jesus, the Lord of scripture and Jesus, the Lord of the Church. It is this vision which rescues both Church and scripture alike from idolatry and superstition. 'The Church to teach, the Bible to prove.'[25]

So Jesus is the Lord of scripture. On the road to Emmaus, we read: 'Beginning with Moses and all the prophets, he (Jesus) interpreted to them in all the scriptures, the things concerning himself'.[26] And again, later in the same chapter: 'Then he (Jesus) opened their minds to understand the scriptures, and said to them, "thus it is written, that Christ should suffer, and on the third day rise again from the dead, and that repentance and forgiveness of sins should be preached to all nations, beginning from Jerusalem. *And you are witnesses of these things*".'[27] In other words it is the task of the living Church to witness to the fact that the living, contemporary Christ is the fulfilment of 'everything' in 'the law of Moses and the prophets and the psalms' (viz verse 44). The outcome of this is always the same experience in the life of the Church. 'It is to men and women, not in vacuo but in the contemporary context of their existence, that the word in the Bible speaks.' So we can also say, with those first disciples, 'did not our hearts burn within us while he opened the scriptures to us?'[28] For the scriptures come alive when they point beyond themselves to their living Lord, the word made flesh, as surely as the Church comes alive when it points beyond its tradition and practices to the unseen Lord in its midst. Both alike do not seek their own glory, but the glory of their Lord.

Yet, the Jesus of Nazareth in the pages of the historical events as recorded in the New Testament is not the complete picture. For the Church must not only bear witness to the fact that Jesus of Nazareth in his life, death and resurrection is the fulfilment of all the yearnings and longings of the old Covenant and therefore the Old Testament, but it must make 'as though it would also go further'[29] and even now while on earth already witness to the Jesus of glory, to the kingdom and to the end of all things. In every sense, the Bible – Old and New Testament alike – cannot be an end in itself, but points beyond itself to him who is beyond everything. In that sense Jesus Christ is Lord of scripture.

So we need to ask: what kind of authority has the Bible? In the first place we need always to talk of scriptures and not a book called the Bible. Unhappily we have a misleading translation from the outset when we use the word Bible as though we are speaking of a book and not of books. 'The Bible', writes Michael Ramsey, 'is the sacred book of the Christian Church. The familiar English word comes from the Greek through the Latin. The Greek original, biblia, meant simply "the books" and when the word was translated into Latin it came to be a singular feminine noun'[30] – not the only thing that went wrong when the Greek and Hebrew scriptures were translated into the Latin of the medieval vulgate translation! So in fact, we are talking of a library of books, written over the course of several centuries. We need to find our way around the Jesus library and to realize that we go to different sections of this library, as with any library, with differing criteria of authority. We do not go to the poetry section and ask the same sort of questions as we do in the history section, and certainly not the same sort of questions as we would ask in the scientific section (which incidentally does not really exist in our sense of the word in any sections of any library covering the centuries in which the Bible books were written). Hopefully, we shall not, therefore, make the mistake of opening the book of Genesis and asking either historical or quasi-scientific questions or by demanding that it is true in that kind of way, any more than we would ask such questions in the poetry or legend section of a contemporary library. It is because in Anglicanism we have not isolated the scriptures and placed them on a pedestal of superstition, and not seen them as speaking to men and women in vacuo, but rather in 'the contemporary context of their existence', that we have not been afraid to apply what in broad terms we might call biblical criticism. We can state unashamedly: 'the tradition of the inerrancy of the Bible commonly held in the Church until the beginning of the nineteenth century (though often held in association with allegorical or other interpretations which profoundly modified its significance) cannot be maintained in the light of the knowledge now at our disposal'.[31] Here again, as in our understanding of the authority of the Church, we do not need to claim inerrancy as the basis of authority. We need not be ashamed to say that both Church and scripture speak with authority – an authority which is in no way undermined because as Anglicans we do not feel able to say that either speaks infallibly. To do so, is to lift both Church and Bible alike out of the common stream of humanity in which also the human experience finds its true authority. 'The faith and doctrine of Christianity are handed down to us in the context of a living fellowship', and that living fellowship need not claim freedom from human frailty in order to discover an authoritative statement of God's infallible self revelation. In Psalm sixty-two there is a possible translation which would read, 'God spake once but I heard two things'! That is always a possibility! The revelation of God in Christ is the ultimate authority,but what he has spoken clearly once, the witness of scripture and the Church alike will frequently blur into two pictures with two or more blurred edges.

So then, in what sense are the scriptures true? 'Without true facts of history, the sacred scriptures will not be what they are.

But to accept this is not to deny that the recording of history may in the scriptures be mingled with symbolic interpretation which itself may be a vehicle of truth. Nor is it to deny that the records may contain details which are not factually correct, for indeed the discrepancies in some of the narratives make the acceptance of them all as factually correct to be virtually impossible. This admission does not, however, invalidate the belief that the scriptures are "true" when we go on to recall that there are other aspects of the truth besides historical fact. The scriptures can convey truth about God and move through poetry, drama, allegory and story. Furthermore, their status lies in their claim to convey "the truth of God"'.[32] Michael Ramsey concludes by reminding us here – as above – that, 'no words, even inspired words, are wholly adequate to convey the reality of God: it transcends the media which conveys it and amongst those media the use of imagery and parable has its place'.[33] In other words, the word is beyond all words, even inspired ones and it is to the word (and to him only) that we attribute inerrancy and infallibility. So it is from that same word that the words of scripture (albeit not free from inerrancy) derive their authority and not their infallibility.

So then, in what sense can we speak of the scriptures as inspired? We need to distinguish here between inspiration and possession. Many of the Reformed Churches and recent biblical sects speak of inspiration as though it were the same as possession. The report, *Doctrine in the Church of England*, is adamant in maintaining a distinction – an important and helpful distinction. 'Inspiration is not to be thought of as analogous to "possession", in which the personality of the possessed is superseded; nor does it appear that its nature can be illustrated by reference to those "physical phenomena" which have recently attracted great interest in many quarters. The truly inspired are those whose response to the Spirit of God has issued in a free surrender to His guidance. In this surrender all individual characteristics of mentality, temperament, knowledge, and the like remain, and when inspiration issues in writing, these characteristics appear in what is written.'[34]

And finally we might well ask in what sense the scriptures

are God's revelation of himself. Revelation is a process not an object. In the process of self-disclosure, God has revealed himself to the people of the old and new Covenants in their history and in the crucial events of their corporate and national life. In some sense, the Bible is a record of those events and reveals to us the nature of God. Yet here again, we need to be mindful of the unique category with which theology is concerned. God, by definition, must be beyond all our definitions and in that sense all revelation is only partial. Try showing to someone who has never seen it, pictures of Chartres Cathedral in such a way as to convey to them the overwhelming grandeur and the power of this huge architectural masterpiece. You will immediately realize the limitations of two dimensions in trying to convey what is after all in three dimensions. You will need differing (sometimes even apparently contradictory) snapshots taken from different angles and varying viewpoints. Neither will you be able to say in quite what order you should place them, nor claim necessarily that the later shots are a fuller representation than the earlier ones. All will be needed and when all is said and done not the half will be told.

So it is with the revelation of God in scripture. There is much which is both primitive and crude, though we must not suppose that the former presupposes the latter. There is much which is apparently contradictory, and we should be very wary of placing one piece of evidence above another or be too ready to eliminate the contradictions, for there will be much which will convey something of what God is by saying in a rather negative way what he is not. Above all, the test and touchstone throughout will be, for the Christian, his understanding of, and in some sense his knowledge and experience of, the person of Jesus himself, as he makes himself known in all the three evidences which we have listed in this book: the word in creation, the word in the Church and the words of scripture. 'God has spoken to us in divers ways . . . but in these last days he has spoken to us by a Son.'[35]

After all, it was from within their knowledge and experience of the risen Christ and his Holy Spirit, that the early Church decided what should be included and what should be excluded

100

in what they came to call the canon of the scriptures. They also were aware of contradictions and difficulties and, although at first some books were included which were later excluded and vice versa, after a while a convergence of opinion gave to the present books of our scriptures an authority which derived from the fact that *these* writings (and not others) rang bells with their corporate experience and knowledge of Jesus the Christ, *within* the worshipping community and the context of the faith of the faithful over many years. In that sense, the Bible is the property of the Church and demands a context if we are to speak of it in any real sense as God's revelation to man. 'The collection of sacred books was not the basis of a belief in a divine revelation, but its consequence.'[36]

Of course, much of what is said here and, indeed, much of what Anglicans teach about the Bible would be unacceptable to many contemporary biblical and fundamentalist sects. It has to be honestly said, that there is a sharp divergence at this point between Anglican teaching about the scriptures and the teaching and beliefs of many other Christians in our day. There are those who give to the Bible an authority *above* the Church. They would say that Article Six of the Thirty-Nine Articles does not go far enough. They would say that nothing can be legitimately thought, said or done by the Christian that is not in the Bible. Furthermore, many such sects would wish to say that every word in the scriptures is literally true and that its authority is derived from the fact that it is totally free from error throughout. Biblicism is a widespread disease in an age hungry for authority. At the outset it appears to be a strong and attractive manifesto, yet in fact, it is in the end an end in itself (a cul de sac), and represents just that very idolatry from which the Bible is itself so at pains to deliver us. There is a literalism and a fundamentalism which would turn to the Bible for the answer to every contemporary problem, even to the precise dating of the end of the world. Anglicans would say that only our Lord and Saviour Jesus Christ is the answer to every contemporary problem and the Bible and the Church are two evidences to help us to draw closer to the mind of Christ: neither can claim to have it in themselves and to possess that mind. The Church to teach, the Bible to prove, and both alike to point men and women to a living Lord who is beyond all as well as in all.

There are, likewise, Christians who place the authority of the Church *above* the Bible. The Tridentine teaching of the Roman Catholic Church did just this, and it is a cause for great rejoicing that this was explicitly corrected (as we saw elsewhere in this book) by the teaching arising out of Vatican II. The official teaching of the Roman Catholic Church is now much more akin to that of Anglicanism and has brought about nothing short of a revolution in the chemistry of catholic liturgy, worship and spirituality. In many ways (and I hope this does not sound condescending) Roman Catholics have now responded to one of the principal challenges of the Reformation with the powerful assertion of the place of scripture in vernacular translations which are now available to the life of the whole people of God – a challenge which reformed and re-shaped Catholicism in the Anglican Church over four hundred years ago. We see now – and it is a cause of great thanksgiving to God – a scriptural Catholicism not only in Anglicanism but also in the Roman Catholic Church with all the fruits which we associate with that kind of spiritual insight.

For 'treat the Bible like any other book and you will find it is not like any other book' (Jowett). The Bible over the past hundred and fifty years has been subjected to the most hostile and rigorous textual criticism ever experienced by any other book in the whole of the world's literature. It stands the other side of that experience today with a renewed and vigorous authority, and is all the more persuasive as a result of that criticism than it could ever have been if religious fanatics had sought to protect its hallowed pages from such critical examination. We have instead allowed it (and Anglicans have been remarkably conspicuous in this particular exercise) to be placed under the scrutiny of every known criteria – we have treated it like any other book (though in practice probably more so) and the end result is that we have found that it is not quite like any other book in the whole world.

During the nineteenth century, especially from Darwin

with his *Origin of Species* through to the present day, Anglican scholarship (with its emphasis upon the place of reason and experience) has brought to bear upon the pages of scripture an exacting and at times ruthless questioning and criticism. At the hands of men of the calibre of Bishop Lightfoot of Durham, Bishop Westcott and Professor Hort, the Bible for Anglicans has been rescued from a protected authority and has emerged after a century with an authority which cannot be taken from it. It is an authority which refuses to retreat from contemporary scholarship and which is therefore all the more robust and reliable because it can now speak to the mind and intellect as well as to the heart and spirit of man. We have had some shocks; and many sacred cows have had to be ruthlessly slaughtered and golden calves have had to be shattered. But the end result is always the same: the death of idolatry and a new beginning in the worship of the true and living God whom no man can see and live. I hope it is not a wrong denominational pride to say that Anglican scholarship has been persistent and conspicuous in this difficult yet ever urgent task, from the scholars of the nineteenth century through to William Temple, Michael Ramsey and John Robinson in our own day.

And still the Bible is a book of presence and a book of power. In all generations and in every age people have opened it and its words have pointed them to the word which in its turn has changed their lives. From the Ethiopian eunuch in Acts to St Augustine and John Wesley, men and women have found in those words the presence of the word made flesh, drawing them through the preached or spoken words to a commitment which radically changed the whole of their lives. In less spectacular ways that has been the daily experience of countless ordinary men and women who have obeyed the command of the voice in Augustine's vision and who have literally picked up that book and read it. Anglicans at the Reformation took the Bible off the shelves of libraries and out of the hands of dusty scholars and picked it up and read it in the context of faith and worship. This great cloud of witnesses from every age would attest to its living and unique authority and would wish to make sure in their own teaching and witness that the scriptures are an essential fibre in the diet of Christian living. 'The light which critical study can bring, the light which comes from the mind and the experience of the Church', concludes Bishop Michael Ramsey, 'these illumine the meaning of the Bible for those who would understand it – but it is to *them* that it speaks the divine Word of love and judgement: "today, if you will hear his voice, harden not your hearts".'[37]

NOTES

1. Charles E. Raven, *Christianity and Science*, United Society for Christian Literature, Lutterworth Press, 1955, p. 18
2. 1 Corinthians 2.16
3. Philippians 2.5
4. H. Richard Niebuhr, *The Kingdom of God in America*, Harper Torchbrook, pp. 191 ff.
5. Charles Williams, *He came down from heaven*, Faber and Faber, 1950, p. 25
6. Titus 1.15
7. C. E. Raven *Teilhard de Chardin, Scientist and Seer*, Collins, 1962, p. 22
8. Romans 8.28
9. 1 Corinthians 1.26
10. Hebrews 1.1
11. *Doctrine in the Church of England*, SPCK, 1938, p. 27
12. J. H. Newman, *An essay on the development of Christian doctrine*, Penguin Books, 1974, p. 100
13. *Doctrine in the Church of England*, p. 35
14. Ibid.
15. A. M. Ramsey, 'What is Anglican Theology' in *Theology XLVIII*, Jan. 1945, p. 5
16. *Sunday Times*, 28 Nov. 1982, p. 1
17. A. M. Ramsey, *The Future of the Church*, Morehouse–Barlow Co. Inc., Connecticut, p. 38
18. *Doctrine in the Church of England*, p. 39
19. viz Christopher Booker, *The Neophiliacs*, Fontana/Collins, 1969
20. William J. Wolf (Ed.) *The Spirit of Anglicanism*, T. & T. Clark Ltd, p. 187

21. J. W. C. Wand, *Anglicanism in History and Today*, Weidenfeld & Nicolson, 1961, p. 56
22. A. M. Ramsey, 'The Authority of the Bible' in *Peake's Commentary on the Bible*, Nelson, 1962, p. 1
23. Ibid.
24. Ibid.
25. viz. J. W. C. Wand, *Anglicanism in History and Today*, pp. 56 ff.
26. St Luke 24.27
27. St Luke 24.46–48
28. A. M. Ramsey, ibid. p. 7
29. St Luke 24.32
30. A. M. Ramsey, ibid. p. 1
31. *Doctrine in the Church of England*, p. 29
32. A. M. Ramsey, ibid. p. 6
33. Ibid.
34. *Doctrine in the Church of England*, p. 30
35. Hebrews 1.2
36. A. M. Ramsey, ibid. p. 6
37. Ibid. p. 7

5. Anglican spirituality – living the Christian life as an Anglican

1. Anglicanism and other denominations and religions

'Einer Molland has attempted to describe Christian communions in terms of one special liturgical day. He associates eastern Orthodoxy with Easter, Lutheranism with Good Friday and Anglicanism with Christmas. The doctrine of the Incarnation has dominated Anglicanism to a remarkable degree.'[1] We have seen how the three reference points in Anglican theology not only stubbornly attribute a place of importance to the Church and its tradition, and to the Bible, but also persistently demand a proper place for human reason and human experience at its deepest and most incisive. At its best this tripartite method of doing theology stems from a deep conviction about the continuity between the order of creation and the order of redemption, recognizing that the presence and activity of the word of God (the *logos*) is common to both. Of course it is important to point out the *discontinuity* between creation and redemption, because entrance into the kingdom is not a *straightforward* matter: 'Flesh and blood cannot inherit the kingdom of God'.[2] There must, in some sense, and at some point, be a definite break with the old, a true conversion and a taking up of the new, but the word of God is nevertheless active by prompting and promise in the old created order, albeit promising what can only be fulfilled in the new order of redemption. Furthermore, because it is the same word of God who is latent in the created order as is manifested and revealed in the redemptive order, we should not be too surprised to find a witness to his way, his truth and his life, however hidden, obscure or even elusive, if we are prepared to dig deep enough into the sub-soil of humanity and humanity's deepest yearnings and aspirations.

At this point, perhaps a word is necessary about the relation between Christianity and other major world religions, including, of course, Judaism. Sometimes, we hear people saying that all religions lead to the same God. There is a truth in that statement, inevitably, but Christianity can, I believe, bring a helpful further perspective to that statement. If we have a strong doctrine of the word latent in all creation in the way that Anglicanism has, then I think we can see a slightly more subtle emphasis in a theology of world faiths which is both embracing in its relationship with other world religions while yet at the same time maintaining the necessarily distinctive elements and contributions which Christianity alone can bring. All yearnings of the human spirit must be drawn, whether in religion, science, art or music, to the word of God in creation. It is surely him to whom all world religions, including Judaism, are being drawn. There are, if it helps to see it this way, lots of different 'old testaments', which are (to borrow St Paul's analogy) 'tutors' which bring us to Christ. As a Christian, I believe, however, that only Christ can present us to the Father: only in Christ, by the action of the Holy Spirit, can we be incorporated into the very life and heart of the Trinity. Such a model, I believe, does not question the religious integrity of all other serious world religions, world philosophy and art, but it also does (and here is necessarily, I believe, the apparent arrogance of Christianity) demand the conversion in Christ of all religion by the activity of the Holy Spirit, if we are actually to enter *into* the fullness and fulfilment of all these yearnings by 'abiding' with the Father in the Son by the action of the Holy Spirit. That is the only place where all the promises will be fulfilled and where we shall reach our rest and true destiny. Here again, there will be a kind of breaking point, without which no man can really hear or receive Christ, reach out or come to know the word made flesh. That is surely the necessary turning point, which in no way invalidates all the past with all that is most worthwhile in it, yet brings that past into its true future – the convergence of all humanity's yearnings when mankind will finally be at home in and with God. The Incarnation and Ascension are two sides of the same truth with Calvary at the crossroads of new commitment and total conversion. *All* religion needs converting: the higher religions need converting most, and Christianity needs the most conversion of all!

2. A spirituality of the Incarnation of Jesus Christ

Nevertheless it is the peculiar and important contribution of Anglicanism to start with its roots firmly incarnated in the soil of all human endeavour, drawing its sap from deep within the recesses of human experience, reason and yearning. Three great Anglican writers have placed on record in their writings the importance of the doctrine of the Incarnation: Bishop Gore, Bishop Temple, Bishop Ramsey. So we shall not be surprised to find the outworkings of this doctrine strongly evident in the spirituality of Anglicanism.

Yet, from the outset, we must be careful, as we have re-marked earlier, how we use that dangerous and ambiguous word – 'spirituality'. In an age of reaction against materialism, the word spirituality can be bandied about all too easily. Try flying the spirituality flag and you will have thousands of fol-lowers of all kinds in no time at all! Yet, in the Christian vocabulary, spirituality does not mean an exclusive concern for only spiritual things. It means, on the contrary, the totality of daily life which the believer is called to live, but seen from the perspective of God. In other words spirituality is con-cerned with the *whole* of material life seen from the perspec-tive of the life of the spirit. St Paul, writing to the Christians in Rome, sees the challenge of spirituality in its protest against the whole outlook of the pagan world. 'Do not be conformed to this world, but be transformed by the renewal of your mind.'[3] This and many other texts show us something of what it is to have the mind of Christ, and therefore in a real sense to possess a Christian spirituality. For spirituality is the ability to see *everything* (matter *and* spirit) through the eyes of the incar-nate Christ and with the mind of Christ. Such an outlook will never be just a trip or an escape: on the contrary it will largely be a matter of plain hard work. It is certainly not a feeling so much as an attitude of mind and a whole outlook on life. It sees no hard lines of division between work and prayer: no

108

yawning gap between the service of the sanctuary and the service of the slum: between sacred and religious, or even between heaven and earth. It is perhaps summed up best in the well known words of that distinctively Anglican writer, George Herbert, in his well known hymn.

> Teach me, my God and King,
> In all things thee to see;
> And what I do in anything
> To do it as for thee!
>
> A man that looks on glass,
> On it may stay his eye;
> Or if he pleaseth, through it pass,
> And then the heaven espy.
>
> All may of thee partake;
> Nothing can be so mean,
> Which with this tincture, 'for thy sake',
> Will not grow bright and clean.
>
> A servant with this clause
> Makes drudgery divine;
> Who sweeps a room, as for thy laws,
> Makes that and the action fine.
>
> This is the famous stone
> That turneth all to gold;
> For that which God doth touch and own
> Cannot for less be told.

Every word of this hymn is a spiritual classic and perhaps you will never find a better place to turn to, to capture something of what the Anglican Christian means by Christian spirituality.

For in Anglican spirituality there is nothing self-consciously spiritual. John Keble, that other great Anglican divine and writer of poetry, and therefore hymns, cautions us and requires that in our spiritual exercises we should not 'Strive to wind ourselves too high for sinful man beneath the sky'. There is necessarily about Anglican spirituality an ordinariness, a lack of self-conscious systems, precisely because, 'The trivial round, the common task would furnish all we ought to ask – room to deny ourselves, a road to bring us daily nearer God'. Those who wish to caricature Anglicanism are always all too easily tempted to point to its flabbiness and lack of apparent zeal and enthusiasm. Those, however, who have found in it a gospel way would remind its critics that almost all the analogies of spiritual growth and maturity on our Lord's lips are horticultural ones. Farmers and gardeners alike are remarkably free from the phrenetic zeal more common to city dwellers and other professions which apparently have far more impressive profiles, precisely because 'the seed grows, he knows not how'.[4] So it is that the placing of books on an index or the official silencing of a speaker are not methods congenial to Anglicans. Another way of describing this trait is to call it the absence of fanaticism.[5] Yet, it is true that 'a communion which places so high an evaluation on sobriety and reasonableness will at times obviously have problems with zeal and conviction'.[6] Nevertheless, Martin Thornton in his great classic, *English Spirituality* writes: 'Empirical guidance, not dogmatic direction: affectiveness, curbed by doctrine; recollection, continuous and gentle, not set periods of stiff devotion; domesticity not militarism; optimism not rigour; all leads naturally into a balance, a sanity, into what Julian called "full and homely" and what Taylor meant by "an amiable captivity of the Spirit"'.[7]

Such is the texture of Anglican spirituality. It distinguishes itself from the rigorism of Calvinism and certain models of Roman Catholic Spanish spirituality such as St John of the Cross and St Teresa of Avila. It is strongly Benedictine in flavour and, not surprisingly, after the strong influence of Augustine of Canterbury, Anselm and Lanfranc – all of whom were early influences upon Anglicanism as well as being conspicuous as followers of the Rule of St Benedict. Scratch both the spirituality of the Prayer Book and the elusive practice of its spirituality amongst Anglicans, and not far below the surface you will find traces of the Rule of St Benedict, with its strong emphasis on corporate prayer and worship, the importance of the place of the laity, hospitality and concern for those on your doorstep and a sanity and balance which permits and encourages an industry of wine making! Calvinism tends to reject the world and the natural order: Roman Catholicism tends to spiritualize the world and its order: in Anglicanism (as in Orthodoxy) there is a readiness to see the whole world as sacrament and to claim the potential within heaven and earth for glory, all waiting to be revealed. So much is this so, that perhaps it might be more accurate to allot the much neglected feast of the Transfiguration to Anglicanism as being (in Einer Molland's sense) the liturgical day most characteristic of Anglicanism and of Anglican spirituality.

It is no accident that many nineteenth century Anglican country parsons were distinguished as local natural historians. It is no accident that at its best Anglicanism has stubbornly pursued a commitment to the social gospel (about which more later) and has taken seriously the counsels of the laity through their 'secular' insights and disciplines in the Councils of the Church. It is sad (and must spring from an unbalanced theology) to watch the Roman Catholic Church formulating its theology almost exclusively from clerical counsels. It must represent a wrong shut-off point from the world of science and the precious insights of a wide spectrum of disciplines. Of course, the Anglican way creates many difficult tensions and presents us with many confrontations and difficulties which we must honestly face in the next chapter, but these are an essential price which must be paid if we are to 'gather up the fragments that remain' that in the end 'nothing be lost' of all God's precious creation.

3. The influence of the Book of Common Prayer

So, from the early Benedictine influence, the Anglican story is proud to point to the medieval and Renaissance witness to spirituality in the writings of Walter Hilton, Dame Julian,

Richard Rolle, Erasmus, and Thomas More (those great Renaissance figures) and then on to Bishop Ken, Bishop Andrewes, John Keble and, in a continuous line, slowly uncovering a living and continuous tradition and witness. Anglican spirituality prefers to do this rather than to point to codified rules and systematic books on spirituality and ascetical theology. From the community at Little Gidding which was, of course, from the outset a lay community, to the writings of T. S. Eliot, Dorothy L. Sayers, Charles Williams, and C. S. Lewis, there has been a strong lay influence – male and female, married and unmarried – and focusing it all, the expression and influence of the Book of Common Prayer which popularized Anglican spirituality to a remarkable, yet subtle and unspectacular degree. 'Public prayer in Anglicanism has, from the mid-sixteenth century, been shaped by one remarkable book. All Churches are made what they are, in a great measure, by their distinctive ways of worship. But the Anglican ethos is peculiar in that so little else shares the central, formative, traditional place that is occupied by the Book of Common Prayer.'[8] In a sense, that is no accident, but rather the inevitable historical outcome of the way in which the Reformation was engineered in sixteenth and seventeenth century England. It is almost as though the English brought the pragmatism of their constitution into their religion and especially into the religious disputes of the Reformation era. Unlike the continental Churches with their lengthy theological confessions, or the Roman Catholic Church with the lengthy dogmatic documents of the Council of Trent, the Anglican Church accompanied each Act of Uniformity in Parliament with a Prayer Book. It was in effect saying something like this: 'If we try to define a clearly demarcated theological position in relation to Rome and Geneva, we shall tear ourselves apart. Here, however, is a living book for living worship. All who feel they can use this book and worship God this way are within the spirit of Anglicanism'. Such an approach meant that within the spirit of Anglicanism, differing theological emphases and outlooks have in fact worshipped together turning to the Prayer Book (and its many revised versions up to our own day) as the source and inspiration for a corporate expression of Anglican spirituality. As we shall see, in the next chapter, these varying emphases have, over the centuries, hardened into parties and the Anglican Communion has certainly not been free from partisan warfare in the rather less impressive chapters of its history. Nevertheless, all have tended to turn to the Prayer Book as a basis for their corporate worship and corporate life and have frequently invoked its order as a vindication for varying patterns and experiences of worship and spirituality. We shall see later, that the rather over-emphasized use of the terms high, middle and low church are an oversimplification and inadequate in their shorthand terminology; yet it must in fact be admitted that it is within the theological and liturgical ethos of the Book of Common Prayer that Christians of very different insights have found a fellowship and world-wide communion.

It is significant that Dean Guthrie defines three kinds of Church in his writings: confessional, experimental and pragmatic.[9] The confessional Church holds that 'what fundamentally makes one part of the Church is one's confession of the faith which is held by the Church'. The second type – experiential – holds 'that what fundamentally makes one a part of the Church is one's having participated in that experience of conversion through which one's fellow Christians came into the body of those who have been saved by Christ. In the understanding of this type of Church, the Church is that body of people who have undergone a common religious experience'. But the Anglican Church, while including elements of both the first and second type is not ultimately defined by either. It is a pragmatic Church: 'It holds that what fundamentally makes one a part of the church is one's doing with the Church what the Church does, liturgically, sacramentally and empirically'.

And so the Book of Common Prayer is a pragmatic book from cover to cover. It does not give a theological treatise on the shape of the ministry, but includes three services for the ordination of the threefold ministry of deacons, priests and bishops. It is not a treatise on various methods of prayer, but emphasizes a strong place for both the Eucharist and the daily offices of the Church with the sturdy implication that the latter are not just for clergymen and should not be muttered like the medieval monastic offices, but should be the daily staple diet of prayer, psalm and Bible-reading open to the whole people of God, summoned to daily corporate prayer by the tolling of the bell. There is no long dissertation on the place of scripture in Christian spirituality, but clearly from cover to cover this is a strongly biblically based book for worship, with huge sections of the scriptures printed out in full for all who can read to read. Many of the divisive issues of Reformation theology therefore are simply avoided by a refreshing emphasis on the practicalities of worship, leaving quite large areas to the discretion of the local Christian community to solve *in practice*.

Naturally for some spirits, this pragmatic approach is all too open to abuse. It drives a John Wesley to the zeal of Methodism where the Church is defined by a common religious experience, and a John Henry Newman to the certainties and tidiness of pre-Vatican II Roman Catholicism, where the Church is defined by a common definition of faith. Nevertheless, the Book of Common Prayer of 1662 and its subsequent revisions throughout the whole of the Anglican Communion up to our own day, have set the feet of Anglicans 'in a large room' with freedom to explore and experiment while at the same time keeping them free from rigidity and uniformity.

4. The priority of scripture in Anglican spirituality: preaching and a Bible spirituality

We are now ready to list the various ingredients which in practice have emerged and have been encouraged in the climate of Anglican spirituality, while realizing that they do not belong to any tidy reference book or confessional document and while also at the same time freely acknowledging that not all Anglicans would be able necessarily to agree equally with all that are listed here. Furthermore, of course, they are not the exclusive property of Anglicans but are shared by Christians of many confessions throughout the world to a greater or lesser extent. Some within the Anglican Church would include and emphasize some elements more than others and would list even some elements which are not stated here: others would wish to soft-pedal or even exclude other elements which this writer sees as part of the whole picture. Here, as elsewhere, we shall find untidy edges and varying shades of emphasis, while still, in some sense being able to distinguish a distinctive picture of what would in general terms be accepted by Anglicans as Anglican spirituality.

So we shall study the chemistry of Anglican spirituality by seeing the respective contributions made to that spirituality by the three main ingredients in the method of Anglican theology which has been the constant theme of this book and which we have traced throughout the whole history of the English Church going back to the very earliest days.

We shall not be surprised to find under the heading of scripture at least three principle ingredients: preaching, Bible study and the daily offices. All the Churches in the west, including the Roman Catholic Church, experienced a revival in preaching in the renewal of the Reformation period. It is not fair to say that such preaching revivals had not been part of the history of the Catholic Church in the west ever since the Church began. The Celtic bishops were great evangelists and the medieval preaching orders – especially the Dominicans and Franciscans – had always placed a special emphasis upon the place of preaching (including outdoor evangelistic preaching). Nevertheless, by the end of the middle ages, the ordinary Catholic parishioner probably was seriously deficient in this part of his diet. Furthermore, such preaching as there was would probably be preaching which exhorted the faithful in their church practices, indulgences and earnest attendance at the sacraments. The distinctive character of preaching arising out of the Reformation insights, which has been distinctive of Anglicanism in the centuries which have followed, has been its biblical basis, in which the content is strongly flavoured with biblical illustrations and texts from Old and New Testaments alike. The result is to create the dialectic of prophecy at the very heart of Christian discipleship, rescuing it from

115

individualistic pietism and giving it a strong element of corporate devotion, especially focused in the person of Jesus. It is still quite common to mount pulpit steps in Anglican churches throughout the world and be met by the stern reminder of a text awaiting you – possibly on the pulpit desk or in a place conspicuous to the eye of the preacher – with the words: 'Sirs, we would see Jesus'. Gospel-centred scriptural preaching has been characteristic of Anglicanism from the days of Dean Colet of St Paul's through to Charles Simeon of the nineteenth century Evangelical revival and Father Stanton and Father Mackay of the more Catholic wing of Anglicanism. At its best, Anglicanism has not seen scriptural, evangelistic preaching as a party option within the Church, but rather as a central responsibility and a challenge to all ministers of the word and sacraments.

Bible study and Bible groups have issued out of this emphasis on scriptural teaching and preaching. The liturgy of the Book of Common Prayer and its subsequent revisions have allotted both to the offices of the Church as well as to the Eucharist, large passages of scripture from both the Old and New Testaments. Any one faithfully following the lectionary of the daily offices and the eucharistic lectionary throughout the Church's year will soon have a very good working knowledge of the whole of the Bible. So it is that the Book of Common Prayer of 1662 is quite explicit in the provision which it makes for a systematic daily Bible-reading in its rubrics concerning the daily office.

The psalms have also been an integral part of the Anglican diet and have given to many faithful Anglicans such a knowledge of the psalms that they have formed part of their personal and spontaneous prayer. Furthermore, at least in the intentions of Cranmer, the offices were intended as the daily diet of the faithful and not simply a clerical responsibility, muttered in the manner of medieval monastic offices. The spirit of the Book of Common Prayer is quite explicit: all priests and deacons are to say daily the morning and evening prayer either privately or openly, 'not being let by sickness or some other urgent cause . . . being at home, and not being otherwise reasonably hindered'; he 'shall say the same in the parish church or chapel where he ministereth, and shall cause the bell to be tolled thereunto a convenient time before he begin, that the people may come to hear God's word and to pray with him'.[10] Such an injunction is probably today more practical than at any other time in history. Unemployment, early retirement, more people living to active old age – all these should and could contribute to a daily cell of laity gathered together each day with their priest for corporate prayer, Bible reading and worship.

5. Church order in Anglican spirituality – bishops, priests and deacons

The tradition and teaching of the Church meant that at the Reformation, Catholic Church order in the Church of England, unlike all the continental reformed churches, or the later churches of nonconformity, was retained intact. The threefold orders of the middle ages of deacon, priest and bishop were retained and episcopacy, as essential to Catholic order and continuity, has been cherished throughout Anglicanism not only within its own life but in all its conversations for unity with other non-episcopal churches. It is true that there would be many and varying interpretations of what was meant by episcopacy among many Anglicans. Some would be prepared to contest that episcopacy was not essential to the Church's order but only belonged to its well-being and would therefore see it as little more than desirable rather than essential. Nevertheless in practice Anglicans have retained the Catholic order of episcopacy which has in the last ditch stand rescued it from mere congregationalism on the one hand and stubbornly contested its claim to be part of the universal Catholic Church of Jesus Christ on the other hand. As we shall see, later on, although lay ministry and varying charismatic ministries are recognized by Anglicanism, it retains a staunch adherence to episcopal order which has rescued it from sectarianism or from being what Dean Guthrie calls a merely experiential Church. Along with episcopacy have been the sacraments as objective and effective means of grace and here again, while there has been a reluctance to indulge in over definition about the sacraments, their number and their precise function, the Church of England at the Reformation set its face against experience as the only sign of efficacy and in a pragmatic and rugged theology, rescued sacramental life from the waves of subjectivism which swept across the continental reformed churches in the sixteenth and seventeenth centuries.

6. The sacraments and Anglican spirituality

In our own day there has been a strong charismatic and pentecostal emphasis in the renewal of Anglicanism, but as in earlier ages of renewal, this has been contained and constrained by a strong doctrine of the givenness of Holy Orders and the objective working of God's grace in the sacraments appropriated (but not limited) by the faith at work in the heart and life of the believer. Experience is important and emotions certainly have a part to play in all spirituality, but there must be checks and balances which prevent the tyranny of feelings or the temptation to define and limit God's activity to recognizable experiences or emotional displays. In its Articles of religion, Anglicanism explicitly refutes the kind of theology of a Church built merely around experiences of this kind (and especially the Calvinism of the sixteenth century) by stating that the 'sacraments ordained of Christ be not only badges or tokens of Christian men's profession, but rather they be certain sure witnesses and effectual signs of grace . . . by the which he doth work invisibly in us'.[11] And again in the next Article, Anglicanism is quite explicit that the 'unworthiness of the ministers' does not 'hinder' the sacraments. There is to be no taking the spiritual temperature either of the priest or of the people! The ordering of the Church is essentially grounded in God's grace – his free, undeserved gift. Furthermore, God is faithful to his promise and his covenants, and the ministry of the Church, its sacraments and its means of grace are rooted in *his* faithfulness and are not determined by *our* wayward faith. In Anglicanism (again unlike

118

some of the Churches of the Reformation) the Church is seen as part of the gospel – part of God's loving gift and generosity and not as something over and against 'real gospel religion'. It is Bishop Michael Ramsey, in one of his early books, who spells this out most eloquently with its resounding title, *The Gospel and the Catholic Church*. So he can write: 'Those who cherish the Catholic Church and its historic order need to expound its meaning not in legalistic and institutionalist language, but in evangelical language as the expression of the gospel of God'.[12] The rejection of the Church as an institution at the close of the middle ages was almost inevitable, because it seemed so remotely related to the sense of good news and gracious givenness which new born evangelical preachers were beginning to expound from the pulpit and experience with their congregations. Both the ordained ministry, the historic episcopate and the sacraments are practical, objective gifts from a generous God to his people, freeing them within a given framework (in which indeed all true freedom on earth is best protected) while not seeking to imprison within any unnecessary formulae the hidden treasure of his love. For we all need rescuing from the tyranny of emotions and spontaneity. Both have a strange knack of becoming engineered and formalist if they are left to themselves with no other checks. There can be something very self-centred and contrived about so-called spontaneous praise! We need the assurance of God's unchanging faithfulness to his promises, within which we can discover both our faith and also be permitted honestly to face our evident and blatant unfaithfulness. The ordained ministry and the sacraments of the Church, rightly understood, belong to that faithfulness, not to our faith, and to his covenant activity, rather than to our good works.

We shall not be surprised, therefore, if in Anglicanism there is a reluctance to extend the limits of essential and saving faith beyond a minimum of dogmatic statements. The Thirty-Nine Articles speak of 'two Sacraments ordained of Christ our Lord in the Gospel, that is to say Baptism and the Supper of the Lord', while leaving room for 'those five commonly called Sacraments, that is to say, Confirmation, Penance, Orders,

119

Matrimony and extreme Unction'. Furthermore, while many things might be believed in the hearts and piety of the faithful over the ages, there is an unwillingness to keep adding peripheral articles of faith to the main essential body of faith which is generally under the heading of saving faith. The Councils of the Church can and do err (viz Article 21) and the authority of the Church to 'decree rites and ceremonies' must be continually checked by reference to Holy Scripture, while freely acknowledging that the Church is (as we have seen earlier) 'a witness and a keeper of holy writ'. In practice, Anglicanism has restricted its essential articles of faith to those details as taught by the early ecumenical Councils of the undivided Church. While Roman Catholicism has added as articles of faith necessary to salvation such matters as the Immaculate Conception of the Blessed Virgin Mary and the bodily Assumption of the Blessed Virgin Mary, Anglicans, like the Orthodox Churches of the east, have freely recognized such belief as part of the experience of the worshipping and praying Church but have not been willing to upgrade such matters of faith to the level of belief 'necessary to salvation'. On the whole, Anglicanism minimizes the extent of its formulae of belief, leaving plenty of room at the edges for matters of faith which may or may not be believed. Jesus cautions us in the New Testament not to lay burdens upon the shoulders of the faithful too heavy to bear and there is surely a pastoral reasoning behind the Anglican refusal to heap up articles of faith beyond what is truly essential to salvation.

All this is especially true in relation to Anglican teaching about the sacrament of reconciliation and penance. Such had been the medieval abuse of this sacrament, that there was a strong reaction against sacramental confession among the Reformation Churches. Here again Anglicanism can be easily caricatured as woolly and not sufficiently sturdy, for although the Book of Common Prayer is quite explicit in its intentions to retain the practice of this sacrament, it sets it within the gospel teaching of assurance. In the Order of the Visitation of the Sick there is deliberate provision made for sacramental confession and absolution ministered by the priest, and the exhortation at the Holy Communion presses home eloquently the importance of this gospel sacrament. Nevertheless, in the end, the formula which Anglicanism has evolved in practice is bluntly stated in the following words: 'All may, some ought, none must'. To many this may well appear as far too open to abuse and as leaving far too many loopholes. But then the object of the exercise is not to trap victims by closing loopholes, but to open men and women to new maturity and more freedom through the freely accepted discipline of the school of charity – the Christian Church. Today, when personal ministry through counselling and the laying-on of hands is much more accepted, amongst many Christians of differing shades of opinion, more Anglicans use this gospel sacrament in a very mature and searching way. At its best, Anglicanism has not driven people from fear to confessional boxes, speaking of mortal and venial sin, but preferred rather to 'sit where they sit' and open the souls of men and women to Christ's healing and generous forgiveness and reconciliation. Reconciliation-rooms of reformed post-Vatican II Roman Catholicism, happily capture something of this spirit of the Anglican practice in relation to this sacrament and represent, along with the ministry of the laying-on-of-hands, a convergence of Christian practice across a wide spectrum of the Churches today. Happily, this sacrament, which for a long time has been divisive among Christians, is now itself a much more reconciling force, providing it is rescued from medieval legalism and related, as it is in Anglicanism at its best, to the place of gospel reassurance, baptism and justification by faith.

7. A eucharistic spirituality

Such also is the case with the place of the Eucharist in Anglican spirituality. By the end of the middle ages, western Catholicism was dominated and perverted by a mentality in which the Mass left little room for other experiences of corporate prayer and worship. The clericalism associated with this mentality inevitably led to the reaction of the Reformation, and many Reformed Churches retained only a corner of spirituality for the Lord's Supper, while altars were banished and pulpits were erected. The Book of Common Prayer, however, kept the centrality of the Eucharist, by seeing it as the characteristic activity of the Church, intended to be celebrated every Sunday and on major feasts. Furthermore, there was a richer diet of alternative services, with a new provision for the place of the word in liturgy and preaching. It has to be freely admitted that, since the Reformation, many Anglicans have marginalized the Eucharist in their spirituality and a proper emphasis upon it as the characteristic activity of God's people has tended to be championed as a party slogan within the Church. Furthermore, for a long time much of the emphasis given to the Eucharist tended to be as a personal and private devotion, retained for the quiet eight o'clock celebration. Two new emphases have changed this picture. First, through such movements within Anglicanism as the 'Parish-and-People Movement' Anglicans have rediscovered a more corporate view of the spirituality which is associated with the Eucharist. Christ's people are the body of Christ and their identity is in some sense related to the person of Jesus Christ and also to the sacrament of the body of Christ on the altar. Secondly, Evangelicals in recent years have explicitly affirmed the centrality of the Eucharist and out of a conference at St John's, Nottingham there has arisen a renewed and vigorous eucharistic spirituality. This is not a party statement, locked in old battles of churchmanship, but is a broadly-based gospel statement appealing to a wide spectrum of Anglican practice. For a long time, it was at the Eucharist – sadly enough intended by Christ to be his sacrament of unity – that party divisions within Anglicanism were most conspicuous and most evident. From the way it was done, to what was worn, it was intended to make a statement about churchmanship – is it high; is it low? If you were a Catholic and high church the Eucharist looked and felt like a Roman Catholic Mass: if you were evangelical and low church the Eucharist looked like a memorial of the Lord's Supper dressed in the outward trappings of sixteenth century puritanism. Thankfully, a real breakthrough of scholarship has within half a century changed this party attitude for all Christians of every shade, colour and persuasion, and in all the Churches a renewed understanding of the Eucharist and its place in Christian spirituality has emerged in recent years. The Canons of Hippolytus were the eucharistic prayers used in the third century. These were unknown to the middle ages and to Cranmer and the reformers. The shape, structure and emphasis of these Canons (eucharistic prayers) have radically affected all the Churches in this century and have given to all Christians today once again a unity of practice and belief about the Eucharist which seemed totally impossible in earlier ages. Furthermore, the Eucharist has become for Christians not so much a service as a whole way of life: we no longer just go to the Eucharist, to Mass or to make our Communion: we seek to live eucharistically – to be a eucharistic people. Anglican eucharistic practice has seldom in its whole history been more unifying and more evidently effective in binding us together not only to partake of the body of Christ in communion but also to be his body in the world. It is this thrust which can be so powerful in a Christian understanding of service and concern for God's world, as we work out increasingly the remarkable insight of St Paul in 1 Corinthians 12 with the staggering realization that to be a Christian is indeed to be a member and limb of the body of Christ, continuing in the world today the same works (and even greater works) of redemption as Christ himself wrought in his own earthly ministry. It is a huge and challenging vision, which rescues Christian spirituality from both individualistic piety on the one hand and clerical domination on the other. The miracle of God's grace is nothing less than the earth-shattering realization that as Christians meet with each other we are indeed 'the body of Christ'. Central to Christian spirituality is the working out of all the implications of that fact and the incredible adventure of living each day as though this underlying reality were really true.

8. The Church and the world

In all these ways Anglicanism has witnessed to the Catholic

practice and ordering of the ministry, an authority of the Church (about which more in the next chapter) and the sacramental life from within an environment which is strongly coloured by scriptural and biblical spirituality. We need now to look under the third element of our tripartite Anglican model at the spirituality implicit in a theology derived from reason and experience. We have seen how Anglicanism emphasizes the continuing activity of the word of God not only in scripture and in the historical events associated with the word made flesh, Jesus of Nazareth, but also in the created order. Inevitably, this has led to a cherishing of the created order in a way which was totally alien to many of the Reformed Churches at the Reformation in general and to Calvinists in particular. If you believe, as Calvinists do, that the whole created order is totally depraved, then you will not be seeking much rapport or dialogue between the word of God in the created order and within the processes of redemption. Such a view will only seek to emphasize that the world is evil and must be written off as secular. It is most unfortunate that the New Testament uses two different Greek words for which the English in most versions only has one word – 'world'. One Greek word (*cosmos*) means the created order, matter and all that God has made: the other word means the passing age, the vogue of secularism. We are told in St John to hate the world and here the writer means the passing age – that which is truly secular. But we are also told that God so loved the world (the created order) and the whole experience and reason of mankind within that order, however scarred by sin. For we shall hold on to the ultimate fact that the created order still retains something of its resemblance to the God who created it and to his truth, way and life.

If this is so, we shall cherish the insights which come from lay insights and lay disciplines. That is the Anglican position. It does not – at its best – use the word 'lay' to mean second class. It involves the laity in the councils of the Church. It believes, and is increasingly developing today an all-member ministry, which involves every baptized man, woman and child. Of course, this can fall into the trap of copying (in a secondhand way) the world's view of democracy. A living theology, however, will transcend mere democratic tokenism and present the vision of a whole orchestra of diverse ministries, held together by the overseeing ministry of the episcopacy whereby unity is preserved in the bond of peace. And then (and scripture is eloquent in its support for such a view), there will be a strong element in a spirituality fed by reason and experience of concern for the wider society, not only in the poor, the hungry, the Third World and injustice (for Christ tells us that he is *in* them); but there will also be a stubborn persistence to make sure that the need to wrestle with the concerns of the world in everything from the environment to the question of nuclear weapons forms part of the continuing agenda of the Church's concerns. It is no accident that it was the Anglican Church in its synod of York and Canterbury which promoted one of the finest debates on record on the question of 'The Bomb' and that it should capture the world media both with the excellency of that debate and by the report out of which the debate arose. Furthermore, when Parliament redebated in 1983 the possibility of the introduction of capital punishment for certain crimes, it is significant that the Church of England General Synod debated the day *before* Parliament's debate, and had a real influence on the outcome of this debate not only in the House of Commons but in the nation at large.

For, at its best, Anglicanism has had a strong theology of the kingdom and has always irrigated a 'churchy' spirituality with the wider and transcending concerns of that kingdom. Once again we see how easy it is to caricature the Church of England as being merely a part of the establishment – Erastian – a mere department of the State. Historically it was inevitable that the Church of England at the Reformation would continue the medieval close relationship with the organs of secular government and the established institutions of the society in which it found itself. It must not be forgotten, however, that the Church of England is unique in Anglicanism at large in this particular way, mainly because of the historical accidents of the sixteenth and seventeenth century English society.

Still to this day, the Queen and Prime Minister have a special relationship to the Church of England. It is no longer true to say, however, that they choose the bishops. An elaborate system ensures that both of them are involved in the process which chooses the bishops, and the Queen, as Supreme Governor of the Church of England, must give her consent to all such appointments. In practice, however, the choice is in the hands of the Church – clergy and laity – and is no more influenced by the State in this respect than anywhere else in the world and nothing like as much as in the Roman Catholic Church of the middle ages was in the hands of the State for a large part of its history.

Yet the abiding reality behind the historical shadow of the Establishment – and this is common to world-wide Anglicanism – is a spirituality which refuses to allow it to be just a *gathered* Church, unconcerned with society at large and with worldly matters in general. Our theological mandate forbids such a sectarian view, and challenges our members to be actively concerned in the events and concerns of the world as part of their Christian spirituality. Perhaps most conspicuous in this has been the resolute and brave opposition by the Anglican Church in South Africa against the apartheid policies of the state in that country.

The place of reason and experience in the Anglican model has, however, brought other characteristics to Anglican spirituality which are certainly worthy of mention and which in a longer book would deserve far fuller treatment. There is at the heart of Anglican spirituality, a healthy agnosticism and a bewildering flexibility. Many moral issues, from contraception and birth control to homosexuality and pacifism, are part of a continuing debate for Anglicans and are not subject to an edict mentality in which the decision is made from the top and an absolute ruling is given. It is precisely because we have to listen to the voice of the word, however elusive, in the disciplines of science and medicine which are continuing to develop and change, that the Anglican does not feel that his faith can give him firm and final answers to these and many other vexed questions of the day. To many, such apparent untidiness is a real stumbling block. Many would prefer the model of the ranks of an army in step to the straggling line of Canterbury pilgrims in Chaucer's tales, evidently at various stages of their pilgrimage, as the model of their membership of Christ's Church. Yet surely a living spirituality must take account of the many and different ways in which different people find and follow the one Christ, working out in everyday life his claim upon them and their responsibility to witness to his love and judgement in everyday concerns.

9. The heart and the emotions within a full spirituality

Finally, one further word about that flexibility of which we spoke earlier. It is because Anglicans cherish a place for human experience and all that it can mean, while checking it and hopefully saving it from the tyranny of individualism and emotionalism, that they have always kept a place for the religion of the heart. Affective prayer and devotion to the name of Jesus; the extended family and the lay community; speaking with tongues and enthusiasm, hymns and singing and music – all these have had a place within the framework of Anglican spirituality. At its best, it has been able to contain the froth of religious experience though it must freely be admitted that it was its rigidity and unresponsive attitude to John Wesley's renewal movement which drove out many Anglicans renewed by the Spirit and by scripture into what later history has called Methodism.

So, in the end, the ultimate test of the theological method of the pudding of Anglicanism is whether, when it is eaten, it can be the diet of a spirituality which can make saints. Each is consequent upon the other: the theological theory is the egg in which the spirituality is formed: the spirituality is tested by the sturdiness of the new born Christian and whether he will live, develop, grow and be changed from glory into glory and ultimately into total conformity with the mind of Christ. As we have said earlier, Anglicans do not (and here again is that untidiness of which we have frequently spoken) formalize their recognition of the saints. It is perhaps typical of the

Roman Catholic Church, with its emphasis on law and order, that it should practise a precise and detailed method of recognizing holy men and women. Anglicans rely upon the lasting substantial consensus of history to pick out men and women in whom the spirit of Christ has been manifest and evident. Such was Edward King, Bishop of Lincoln from 1885 to 1910, and he along with many others now have an informal place in our annual calendar of devotion. For it is the lives of the saints which are the ultimate vindication of all our strivings after right belief and faithful devotion and service. They are a reminder to the whole Church of the ultimate destiny of the whole created order, that in Christ, through grace and conversion, we are all intended to enter into and upon the inheritance of the sons and daughters of the living God.

For in the end we are justified by faith and not by works. The continual and continuous temptation to the Anglican spirit, in so far as it is closely related to something which we call English, is to turn pragmatism into works and to topple over into a Pelagianism which will sit all too lightly to right belief, in the mistaken conviction that in the end it does not matter very much what you believe as long as you try to do the right thing. The opposite of course is the great affirmation of scriptural Christianity and indeed of the whole of life. When days are dark and failure is evident at many levels, it is to the vision of faith that we must turn, and by which in the end we will be justified. There is a strength in refusing to define too clearly the formulae of Christianity and in so far as that is a virtue, Anglicanism has borne witness to it – for such definitions all too easily grow into dogmas which overnight rapidly become idols. Of course on the other hand, there are also real dangers hidden in woolliness and ragged edges, because sooner or later someone will call your bluff and ask you where, if anywhere, you really are compelled to draw the line. When does flexibility become just plain fuzziness: when does pluralism degenerate into that position in which anyone can believe anything? It is to these pressing and contemporary questions that Anglicans in general now need to address themselves, and to which this particular essay now inevitably points us.

NOTES

1. William Wolf (Ed.) *The Spirit of Anglicanism*, T. & T. Clark Ltd, 1982, p. 178
2. 1 Corinthians 15.50
3. Romans 12.2
4. St Mark 4.27
5. William Wolf, ibid. p. 177
6. Ibid.
7. Martin Thornton, *English Spirituality*, SPCK, 1963, p. 302
8. William Wolf (Ed.) *Anglican Spirituality*, Morehouse–Barlow Co. Inc., Connecticut, 1982, p. 105
9. Ibid. p. 3
10. 'Concerning the Service of the Church', Book of Common Prayer, 1662
11. Article XXV
12. A. M. Ramsey, *The Gospel and the Catholic Church*, Longmans, 1936, p. 8

6. What sort of future is there for Anglicanism?

1. Comprehensiveness?

'Catholic we are; Protestant and Reformed we are. Yet also the Renaissance is in our blood, and this made for a saving dose of scepticism, for an openness of mind, for a willingness to suspend judgement until we have more data . . . More important than any formal statement of that consensus of the faithful, more significant than any kind of confessional declaration, is the appearance of a type of human being the world does not otherwise see. He is the Anglican. He creatively synthesizes within his own being the best that is in Catholicism, the best that is in Evangelicalism or Protestantism, the best that is in Liberalism.'[1]

It all sounds very grand, but does he? And furthermore does it work? It might be more honest to say that Anglicanism at its bests *seeks* to synthesize the elements of which this book has spoken from cover to cover. In practice, the synthesis is seldom in evidence. For in practice over the years, and especially recently, the three elements have tended to break down into parties within the Church and to shut their ears to the reflections arising from the other parties in open conflict with them. The tripartite model seems like Humpty-Dumpty to be in bits and pieces, and Anglicanism, if it is to make a proper contribution in worldwide Christianity, seriously needs to put its own house in order first.

This task must really be based upon a living conviction that the theological model of Catholic, Liberal and Evangelical (for the want of better words and for shorthand purposes) is not simply an accident of Anglican history or that cohabitation is making a virtue of necessity. It must not be enough simply to believe that the winds of history have caused a shipwreck and thrown the survivors on to a desert island, on which three different kinds of people survived, and in the name of survival

130

have somehow or another been compelled to learn a toleration for each other. Comprehensiveness, if it is just another name for tolerance, is little better than compromise – insipid and in the end repugnant to all three palates! The belief upon which a living comprehensiveness must be based is in the conviction that without the three ingredients the resulting chemistry, far from being the elixir of eternal life, will be a synthetic mixture and an unbalanced diet.

Peter Baelz, the Dean of Durham, has recently written on this very topic most helpfully. He sees that all three contributors – Catholic, Evangelical and Liberal – need saving from their own strengths, because each insight must be under God and is necessarily less than the whole truth. He writes: 'Neither the scriptures, nor the traditions of the Church can be given that ultimate and unquestioned authority which belong to God alone. Biblical and ecclesiastical fundamentalisms are as idolatrous as they are irrational. If the special temptation of the liberal tradition is to echo without criticism the voice of the present age, the special temptation of both the catholic and evangelical traditions is to echo without criticism the voices of previous ages.'[2] He continues in his conclusions on the nature of comprehensiveness: 'The work of discerning the doctrine which sets forth the life in Christ demands from Christian disciples all the powers of insight, intellect and conscience which they can bring to the task. Because God graciously respects the humanity of those to whom he gives himself, while at the same time remaining infinitely beyond their grasp, there is bound to be a many-sidedness to the apprehension and expression of the gospel. The need for comprehensiveness in the Church derives therefore from a proper recognition of the complementarities of the Christian response to the gospel, not from an easy-going accommodation and compromise'.[3]

Put more succinctly, 'what is required by the very nature of the dialogue is not compromise for the sake of peace, but comprehension for the sake of truth'. Left to themselves the insights of Catholics and Evangelicals alike in Anglicanism tend to degenerate into an enthusiasm and even a fanaticism which is less than the whole gospel. They both alike need to enter the environment of the laboratory for testing from history, scholarship, reason and so-called secular experience, precisely because Jesus Christ is lord of history as well as lord of the Church. Again and again in the Old Testament, the insights of Judaism came from an imposed dialogue between Judaism and its *'enemies'*; for the calling's snare of a religion which is untested by reason, and a revelation which is unchallenged by speculation, is that it inevitably degenerates into what can only be called in the end sheer religious 'humbug'. Again and again in the New Testament, it is just this blinkered outlook which draws from Jesus his strongest condemnation. Futhermore, in fact it is the blatant inhumanity and insensitivity of both unchallenged Catholicism and Evangelicalism alike which the concerned and searching humanist finds such a scandal and stumbling block in history and in his own personal quest.

Equally it must be said, that Liberalism as a thing in itself, enthrones human reason and makes it the ultimate arbiter of everything. Speculation needs to be challenged with the hard realities of revelation and needs to be continually redeemed from the hardness of head and heart alike by the apparent foolishness of the Cross and the inevitable need for a total conversion of the total personality. For as Peter Baelz would wish to remind all Liberals: 'Common sense is no substitute for the gospel, rationalism no substitute for revelation, progress no substitute for providence, education no substitute for conversion and man no substitute for God'.[4] We have seen what happens when the Liberal contribution holds sway and plays tyrant, so that in the end the result is little better than when Catholics or Evangelicals usurp the same position and come into control. The end product is just the same idolatry, but this time not of the Church or the Bible but of reason and the limitations of finite humanity.

For in the end true comprehensiveness is not a little bit of all three, nor is it the via media – a middle of the road Church. It is the continuing tension within the heart of every believer. As Bishop Mervyn Stockwood used to say: 'I count myself lucky that I can believe two seconds out of every three!' Com-

132

prehensiveness is the process of individuation (to use Jung's phrase) in the heart of every believer. Of course by temperament, background and psychological makeup, we shall find ourselves naturally drawn to one or other of the three Rs (Reformation, Renaissance or Counter-Reformation) – Evangelical, Liberal or Catholic – but that must only be the *starting* point for the journey. Growth will always be the reaching out in risk from one's own entrenched position and being caught up in the continuing debate of the heart and of the mind. If Anglicanism breaks down into parties and the parties become gravely at war with each other, then in the end Anglicanism will be condemned to stagnation and fragmentation. So Bishop McAdoo reminds us: 'Seventeenth century Anglicanism, taking it by and large, saw no solution to the problem of authority which did not admit of the mutually illuminating relationship of scripture, antiquity and reason and refused any solution which insulated authority against the testings of history and the free action of reason. It must be such an authority which can stand investigation and command freely-given adherence. It must evoke rather than repress the response of the individual and refuse to pronounce on matters that are not essential'.[5]

Of course our Christian friends from other communities sometimes look on aghast! The Orthodox Churches demanded in 1968 that the Lambeth bishops at their meeting should come clean and agree that comprehensiveness was little more than a sophisticated word for compromise and the refusal to be committed to specific truths. The reply of the Anglican bishops is worth printing in full: 'Comprehensiveness is an attitude of mind which Anglicans have learned from the thought-provoking controversies of their history. We are grateful to the Orthodox for making us think once more what we mean by comprehensiveness, and shall be glad to study the matter afresh with their help; for we realize that we have been too ready to take it for granted. We offer the following reflections to aid discussion. Comprehensiveness demands agreement on fundamentals, while tolerating disagreement on matters in which Christians may differ without feeling the necessity of breaking communion. In the mind of an Anglican, comprehensiveness is not a compromise. Nor is it to bargain one truth for another. It is not a sophisticated word for syncretism. Rather it implies that the apprehension of truth is a growing thing: we only gradually succeed in "knowing the truth". It has been the tradition of Anglicanism to contain within one body both Protestant and Catholic elements. But there is a continuing search for the whole truth in which these elements will find complete reconciliation. Comprehensiveness implies a willingness to allow liberty of interpretation, with a certain slowness in arresting or restraining exploratory thinking. We tend to applaud the wisdom of the rabbi Gamaliel's dictum that if a thing is not of God it will not last very long (Acts 5.38–39). Moreover we are alarmed by the sad experience of too hasty condemnation in the past (as in the case of Galileo). For we believe that in leading us into the truth the Holy Spirit may have some surprises in store for us in the future as he has had in the past'.[6]

2. The place of conflict and consensus

In all of this process, however, there is bound to be conflict. Conflict rightly understood is a sign of health and not sickness. The human body when it is healthy is containing many such conflicts. So it must be with the life of the Church. 'Because the decisions involved in change rest upon judgements, which are necessarily controversial, it is essential to the health of the Church, that it learns how to conduct controversy constructively and openly. Authority is not embodied, it is dispensed: and the reaching of authoritative decisions is a continuous process involving all the participators.'[7] It is important, however, to distinguish partisanship from conflict. Conflict is what is happening when all parties concerned are continuing to hear as well as to speak and are ready to allow the battle to move continually on to new ground with new and changing slogans and passwords. Partisanship means that all the parties concerned are no longer in touch with the opposing forces and that they are only really repeating speeches and slogans – so entrenched that there can be no movement of the debate. 'It is, I believe', writes Stephen Sykes, 'one of the chief weaknesses of the documents of the Second Vatican Council that it conspicuously fails to expect conflict in the Church.'[8] That statement, if it is true, is sad, because conflict is at the heart of music and in many ways it is the dialectic of all harmony and the ultimate resolution of all cadences. An entrenched citadel-mentality which sees effective authority as repressing and silencing conflict is indeed not only a temptation to the Church but one of the continuing issues facing our whole world at the present time.

That is why this discussion is not just a piece of ecclesiastical wrangling. The question of authority is top of our twentieth century world's agenda. Many might say, however, that although the niceties of Anglican theological methods were historically interesting and worked in the seventeenth century, the twentieth century climate both in the Church and in the world is more abrasive and will no longer permit such academic and rarefied discussions. What will be its appeal to the man in the street, if any? Is such a Church condemned inevitably to be the Church of the middle classes, of the readers of the *Guardian*, the white collar workers and of those who feel at home in discussion groups and cells? Certainly Anglicanism is evidently wide open to such a charge. Yet, all too easily totalitarianism has thrived and thrives today on the unquestioned assumption that the man in the street has no questions to ask or, if he has, that he does not have the wherewithal to ask them. Surely we have seen in totalitarian regimes what happens to the man in the street if authority, clarity of vision, leadership and efficiency become the unquestioned idols. The question of authority and its related brother – conflict – is not just an ecclesiastical question but rather one of the most pressing issues in our world and in the contemporary political climate.

In the Lambeth Conference Report of 1948 once again the bishops were drawn to defend the Anglican method in their statement on authority. In the appendix to that report they speak of a dispersed authority which is mutually supporting and mutually checking and which itself is a life process. They recognize 'God's loving provision against the temptations to tyranny and the dangers of unchecked power'. The Church is not without chapters in its own history when it has suppressed conflict in the name of commitment and exercised 'tyranny' and 'unchecked power'. They have been the cruellest and the most scandalous chapters in our history. Secular totalitarianism is ugly: religious totalitarianism is demonic.

So the defence of Anglicanism must not rest upon any less a foundation than upon a deep conviction that it is through conflict that God draws us to real maturity; that dispersed authority is the way the human body works with a healthy interdependence between the members. Cancer is the tyranny of one cell over others – the claiming of an authority which is self-sufficient and can compel submission and silence from the other cells of life.

It is a particular sadness therefore that in recent years synodical government has tended to move in the retrograde direction of copying the conduct of conflict along party lines and secular democratic governments, with percentages and majorities in view. It was the early trade union movement, and also the Quakers, who pursued a yet more excellent way – the way of consensus. For there must be a sense in which God's revelation to man is inevitable and in some sense irresistible if the climate and conduct of debate is such that all may speak and all may hear. On the contemporary vexed question of women in the priesthood, surely the way forward is by consensus and not by narrowly won majorities. In movements of this kind in history, there will always be ebb and flow, but in the end only a Canute would try to resist the overwhelming direction of the tide. It takes time – and what is twenty or thirty years in two thousand? The chances are that if we are prepared to live with the conflict (and, after all, some provinces of the Anglican Communion have already ordained women priests and we now have the opportunity to observe this experiment and to test it in the New Testament way by its fruits) then the battle will move, and we shall soon be discovering further insights into both the nature of sexuality and the nature of priesthood. Perhaps the least helpful people in such a debate are those who believe that there is no difference anyway between men and women on the one hand or between priests and laity on the other! It is here above all else that we need to be able to recognize, express and contain conflict until it is resolved into a realistic and authentic harmony which is always *beyond* the point at which the debate began. Hopefully the particular debate about women in the priesthood will carry our understanding beyond where any of us are at the moment on the frontiers both of the nature of human sexuality on the one hand and, on the other, the whole question of ministry in the Church and its relation to the ordained ministry of the episcopate and its local expression in priesthood.

Indeed, this book has, I hope, moved in its position as it has gone along. It began by explaining the theological method which historically has evolved in the development of Anglicanism over the centuries. By now, hopefully, it is evident that if the tripartite method of theology (and the spirituality arising out of that theology) is true, there can be no going back either for the sake of tidiness or for the sake of unity for its own sake behind the divisions of the Reformation, the Renaissance or the Counter-Reformation. If we were to seek to put together a Church (God forbid) which edited out any of these three contributions, it could not come to maturity without once again shattering in order to affirm one or other of these vital constituents. Unity is always *beyond* and through conflict and takes the life-giving force of the conflict into the new and fuller order. That is why it is so wrong to speak of Anglicanism as a bridge Church or a via media. That is to see it as a way of temporary expediency – a way of joining up two bits of history. Such an image suggests two opposing and irreconcilable states or parties being joined together. That is joinery not unity! Unity has a dynamic force to it which is related to conflict, precisely because it goes *through* and *beyond* the conflict to some new and even more wonderful creation. The one Church of the future for which Christ prays will have a *pleroma* (a fullness) which no Church at the present time possesses. The chances are that such a Church, if it is really to gather up what history has fragmented, will have to exercise an authority and a theological model not unlike that which history has evolved within Anglicanism. That is a brave and (if misunderstood) conceited and arrogant claim. However, if such a statement is set within the context of the kind of discussion which this book has outlined then, hopefully, it can be made without arrogance or without banging the drum for a revival of denominationalism. For, in the gospel way of seeing things, our most useful insights and contributions are always gifts: gifts given almost when we were least expecting them and given to those least deserving of them. There is only a danger in such characteristics if they are ever seen in terms of privilege and power. They are therefore much better seen in terms of the absurd, the ridiculous and even of the role of the clown. Anglicans – and hopefully not this book – must never take themselves too seriously, for only so might they discover that both God and future history take them quite seriously.

For, in the end, the ultimate question is not so much the need to ask whether Anglicanism works or whether it can be made to work or any of these defensive or purely pragmatic questions. The overriding question with which we must ultimately be concerned is whether the Anglican Church is a gospel Church and therefore if it is true, and teaches, preaches and makes explicit that truth in the lives of its ordinary members.

3. Anglicanism and other Churches

If Anglicanism has that gospel ring of truth about it, ultimately it will find an essential place within the fuller harmony of Christian unity on a *worldwide* scale and will not be content to reassert unity merely within the limitations of national Churches.

This book has been written in the belief that there is an urgent call and a worldwide responsibility for Anglicanism today and tomorrow. 'The times call urgently for the Anglican witness to scripture, tradition and reason alike for meeting the problems which biblical theology is creating, for serving the reintegration of the Church and for presenting the faith as at once supernatural and related to contemporary man.'⁹ There, in a few words, is the challenge for Anglicanism at the close of the twentieth century. Its past credentials which have been very much the constant theme of this book, would certainly seem to be pointing Anglicanism towards a special responsibility in the wider environment of world Christianity and indeed also within the forum of world religions.

This book began on a note of optimism and saw in the contemporary climate signs of new opportunities for speaking of the things of God. It also was not unaware of the pitfalls and dangers within the present situation when fear is so prevalent as the motivation for seeking faith. Such a faith must speak to the whole man and to all men and women in all cultures and at different times. It must be relevant and contemporary and yet it must speak of eternity and things supernatural. It must be flexible enough to be local and indigenous and yet it must avoid anything which is sectarian by affirming what is universal and international. It must be able to speak in many tongues and different tongues yet it must speak of the same truth free of discord and resonating with a rich harmony and counterpoint. In a word it must be catholic, or universal. As things stand at the present time no one Church is truly catholic in that sense. Each seeks to emphasize one aspect of Christian truth at the expense of others. So many attempts at Christian unity, however, have been more conspicuous as attempts at joinery: the taking of different shaped blocks and trying to join them together. In such an exercise it is the odd shapes of particular eccentricities and traditions which most get in the way and the temptation is to seek a unity which is based on minimum requirements and less intensive colourings.

This book is written in the belief that there is another way forward: it is the way of setting unity within something greater than itself, and achieving it (not exactly incidentally, but certainly not too self-consciously) on the way to this greater goal. Père Congar speaks helpfully of a new plenitude for all the Churches and gives a different picture and vision for our strivings towards unity. 'For him (the ecumenical worker) the aim is to help other Christian communities and . . his own Church also to approach and converge upon the plenitude which lies before us in the light of which integration will really be able to take place. It is of little importance here to know whether this point of convergence is eschatological or belongs to history'.[10] All the varying Christian communities should, 'correct their deviations ... and pursue their evolution towards the totality of truth and converge upon that point of plenitude which the Catholic Church may not yet have attained'.[11] Unity in that vision is a point of convergence which is a plenitude *beyond* where any of the present Churches are at the present time. Our eyes, in other words, like those of a good driver at Hyde Park Corner should not be too anxiously set on what is behind, or even alongside (though courtesy and commonsense would demand some attention in these directions). Rather we should be looking straight forward to where we are intending to go and indicate accordingly. Unity as an end in itself will then be overtaken by the dynamics of renewal and each and every Christian community will bring to the point of convergence the riches of its own tradition, which will not then be necessarily seen as contradictory or in conflict (as they have been inevitably further back in the race) but rather now as contributing to a fuller (*pleroma*) expression of truth, belief and worship.

In so many ways, Anglicanism has latent within it just these structures and checks and balances which mark it out as a Church which should be conspicuous in this sort of race. Already within our tradition, there is a kind of *pleroma* and diversity. We have been able to hold together (just about) the riches of the faith and order of the Catholic Church, while also retaining the freshness which that immediacy of approach to God through Christ gives in the witness of Evangelical and even charismatic insights. Alongside all of this we have retained a freedom of intellectual enquiry. It is true, as we have seen, that often these three ingredients have failed to pool their contributions and have fragmented into parties within the Church. Nevertheless, at their best, the three constituent elements within Anglicanism have not always been static blocks of protest, but rather have been dynamic contributions to a rich chemistry of a colourful and tasty casserole. For in truth, it must be firmly said, that unity in the early Church was not a question of trying to put pieces of Humpty-Dumpty together in such a way as to keep his balance on the wall, but was the healthy and inevitable problem of a lively Church filled with the Holy Spirit in which the diversity of rich and varying gifts demanded an oversight which would keep the unity of the spirit in the bond of peace.

In this whole movement forward, I believe that true episcopacy which has shed the prelacy of the middle ages or even of nineteenth century Victorian England will be seen to have a vital role to play. Bishops at their best are there to take care of just those very kinds of irregularities which are inevitable in any living and developing organism. There must always be a place for contradiction in all our schemes of theology. Let us daily thank God for Eldad and Medad in the Old Testament: they should be made the patron saints of all scholarly theologians! A college of bishops, properly used, can take care both of local irregularities and also ensure and maintain the wider view of unity. For unity is not a concept or an organizational structure. It belongs to the whole body, pervading it yet not possessed by it, in precisely the same way as health belongs to the whole body and yet is never the property of any one part of it. Health is not a thing in itself. It is an elusive attribute which is most clearly evident when all the parts are working properly and when all the various tensions and checks and balances are at play. In such a concept or image the place of the head is crucial, but headship here not seen (as in so many secular images) as tyranny or authoritarianism, but rather as the servant of the co-ordination of the whole body. (For if the head dominates, the body by definition will certainly not be healthy: such is the reason why scholars need so much help to become human beings!)

Under the oversight of episcopacy (and here the scriptures are at pains to distinguish the difference between oversight and overbearing) local covenanting can be a real way forward. It can afford to be much bolder wherever the oversight is most apparent: the more local the bishop, perhaps the more daring and even more anomalous can be the practice of the local covenant. It will require two things.

The bishop must himself be loyal and faithful and take the strain and tension of local anomalies where it can best be held: in the wider college of bishops. Secondly, anomalies and irregularities can abound best when the norm is clearly stated and where there is not an attempt to rewrite the rules and bring them into line with the latest irregularity. In this case, as in so many others, the exception proves the rule.

This must now be the way forward – and certainly in the Church of England in relation not only to local covenanting with the Roman Catholic Church, but especially with the Nonconformist and Free Churches. Most of the emphases in their traditions which led them to break away from Anglicanism in the first place should, in a healthy Anglican Church, have found a real place, if that Church has been sufficiently renewed in its own credentials. Most of what they subsequently protested against were largely the accidents of the particular sociological and historical structures of the day. The way forward to that *pleroma* and richness of which Père Congar speaks is for each Christian community to arrive at the point of convergence and persistently speak *only* of those things which they wish to affirm, remaining silent about those things which they are against. Thus the agenda at the point of convergence would be reaffirmation of many insights which in the past have divided us. Some would be for an all-member ministry; others would be for various charismatic ministries; others would be for a stronger and more robust doctrine of the Bible; others would wish to set the place of lively liturgy high on the agenda. All of these would be affirmations. There would be no place to hear what we are against! So much of what we have been against has been clothed in the accidents of history. Much opposition to episcopacy has rightly been because that episcopacy in many ages was seen as prelacy. Much opposition to priesthood and the other ordained ministries has justifiably arisen because in the past it has been a package deal with clericalism. Renewal has moved the argument along and we need to follow it and to make sure that we are not simply rehearsing divisions of the past or the reasoning of the past. Hopefully, we shall find that many of these affirmations are not so exclusive or divisive as they appeared to be in their original historical setting.

For we need to learn from recent attempts at unity schemes (especially in the Church of England) that perhaps great national 'joinery' projects which seek to bring together large blocks of institutional Christianity tend to fall apart at the last minute. They are too static in their approach. The sixties and seventies were a time when such schemes appeared to be the way forward. The eighties, I believe, hold out a different promise. Wherever renewal is strong, unity seems to grow and develop almost inevitably – not least where there is a healthy climate of mission and evangelism. When we have gone for unity first, and made this an end in itself, we seem to have lost many precious opportunities for enrichment, renewal and mission. 'Seek first the kingdom of God and his righteousness and all these things' (yes, perhaps even unity) 'shall be yours as well.'[12] We most not select and isolate one of the four attributes of the Church from the creeds (unity, holiness, catholicity and apostolicity) and make it an idol and end in itself.

Dare we look at a larger map of the world and seek our calling as Anglicans on that sort of scale? Yes, I believe we can and I believe we must. 'All Anglican Churches, however, are one in their conscious endeavour to preserve the apostolic faith and character of the church's worship of the first centuries, though trying to incorporate in it the contributions of the Reformation and those of their own time so far as they have positive and permanent value. This typical Anglican attitude in respect of tradition and enrichment is at the basis of the moderation and comprehensiveness of Anglicanism. It marks world-Anglicanism as being, as it were, a provisional prototype of the reunited *Ecumene*, the world Christianity of the future. That Anglicanism comprises only a small number of Christians does not detract from that fact.'[13] Those words, written by a Roman Catholic, do bring great hope, but also present a formidable challenge. It will require boldness of faith, and maturity of mind to hold many of the tensions which are inevitable within the *pleroma* of a richly diverse Catholic community. Yet surely there is no other way to be truly Catholic: anything less is sectarian. For not only must Christ be seen eventually to be the head of his body the Church, but he longs also to be seen as the fulfilment of all the promises of all the religions. Jesus Christ is not the property of the Church: He is the lord of the universe. How can we present him, or rather enable his voice to be heard in the forum where the voices of other world religions are conspicuous and eloquent? It will not be done, with the caution of a sectarian or denominational spirit. The Catholic Christ must be vindicated not only in the fulfilment of Judaism, but also as the fulfilment of Hinduism and Buddhism, not because in the end all religions are true, nor because some religions are not better than others, but because the word was made flesh, according to Christian belief and is latent and hidden in every atom of the universe: he is the light which enlightens the whole human race, and every persistent and recurring religious insight throughout history. In such a world debate I cannot believe that there will not be a place for a 'pope' for all Christians. It may well be that the one who is prepared to be the servant of all could well be an indispensable shepherd to all. By his service (reflecting the servanthood of Christ) he could well bring just that unity and catholicity to Christian faith which will equip it for its last and most important dialogue. For it would seem that the evidence of history would teach us that a unified Church will demand a sacramental sign and focus of that unity *within* (and not above) the worldwide college of bishops. Is it in that sense that we might well speak of a pope for all Christians? Yet in saying all of this, Anglicans would not need to deny other vital ingredients in their distinctive witness – those very ingredients of Reformation witness and Renaissance insight which Anglican history has stubbornly proved can exist (and indeed must exist) alongside Catholic conviction concerning church order and the sacramental life.

'That Anglicanism comprises only a small number of Christians does not detract' from its place as a provisional prototype of the reunited world Christianity of the future. If that is so it is a great calling indeed. It is the conviction that it may well be so which has been behind the writing of the words of this book.

Indeed many would wish to see from the testimony of scripture itself that God's hand has often been most effective in history in precisely those areas of small numbers, frequently delighting to use the small right number of right people in the right place at the right time. Indeed one whole area of the theology of election could well be described in that way. Could it be that Anglicans are such a people and that the time is already ripe because it is now?

NOTES

1. E. R. Fairweather (Ed.) *Anglican Congress 1963*, Seabury Press, New York, 1963, p. 232
2. Peter Baelz, 'Reconsidering Anglicanism's interdependent traditions', *The Times*, 27 November 1982
3. William Wolf (Ed.) *The Spirit of Anglicanism*, T. & T. Clark, Ltd, 1982, p. 154
4. Peter Baelz, ibid.
5. H. R. McAdoo, *The Spirit of Anglicanism*, Adam & Charles Black, 1965, p. 410
6. *The Lambeth Conference 1968*, SPCK & Seabury Press, 1968, pp. 140–41
7. Stephen W. Sykes, *The Integrity of Anglicanism*, Mowbray, 1978, p. 99
8. Ibid. p. 88
9. A. M. Ramsey, *Gore to Temple*, Longmans, 1960, p. ix
10. Yves Congar, *Dialogue between Christians*, Geoffrey Chapman, 1966, p. 95 f.
11. Ibid.
12. St Matthew 6.33
13. W. H. Van de Pol, *Anglicanism in Ecumenical Perspective*, Duquesne University Press, Pittsburg, 1965, p. 34

7. The shape of things to come

1. Christianity in a post-Christian era

In this last chapter, it is surely not inappropriate to permit ourselves to raise our eyes from the past and present and to move to the more elusive skyline of the future, with all its necessarily unpredictable features and to try to sketch, at least in outline, the shape of things to come. Of necessity, a book concerned primarily with Anglicanism could well be accused of being somewhat domestic and sheltered in its concerns – preoccupied with past chapters of history in which Anglicanism has held a somewhat unrealistic place (at least by contemporary standards) in society and in the restricted environment of the western, largely English-speaking world. As our world shrinks through faster travel and more efficient techniques of communication and as the western world takes its place within the larger perspective of other larger groupings on our planet, Christianity finds itself brushing shoulders with other world religions, unprotected by its special history and by the privileges of the established structures of society as surely as the man in the street daily brushes shoulders with the multi-cultural and multi-ethnic society in which so many of us now live. 'What is the place of Christianity in such a world-wide community?' That is to ask a far- reaching question. 'What is the place of *Anglicanism* in such a community?' That might well be seen not so much as asking a far-reaching question as to be asking an absurd question. Nevertheless, however inadequately we are able to reply to such a question, it must surely be the right conclusion to such a book as this: to look forward to the future. Such a decision might even help to deflect, at least a little, any charges of smugness or domesticity which might justifiably be directed against earlier chapters.

People speak – or at least clergymen and theologians frequently speak – of a secular age. It has become the almost unquestioned coinage in the vocabulary of many Christian theologians and speakers and writers today. We are given to believe that – especially in western society – we are now entering a secular age in which there is not only an inability for secular man to understand the language and practice of a supernatural religion, but a positive hostility to any expression of religious beliefs either in worship or in the presentation of those beliefs in ethical and moral issues affecting our contemporary world.

Thankfully, against this majority viewpoint, there is also a minority of questioning voices along with whom the author of this book would wish to raise his own voice of questioning protest. It is simply not true that in stark contrast with medieval man or with more primitive societies, twentieth-century man suddenly is a creature with only a secular outlook. For too long it has been the almost unquestioned assumption by many writers and theologians that primitive is the same as religious, and modern is the same as secular. As the anthropologist, Mary Douglas, shows, this is a gross and misleading over-simplification. 'Secularization is often treated as a modern trend, attributable to the growth of cities or the prestige of science, or just to the breakdown of social forms. But we shall see that it is an age-old cosmological type, a product of definable social experience, which need have nothing to do with urban life or modern science . . . The contrast of secular with religious has nothing whatever to do with the contrast of modern with traditional or primitive. The idea that primitive man is by nature deeply religious is nonsense. The truth is that all the varieties of scepticism, materialism and spiritual fervour are to be found in the range of tribal societies.'[1] It is true that Mary Douglas's thesis does place an emphasis on the place of close relationships and clearly defined roles in society as being precisely those areas in which ritual and the cult have a place, while in contrast a more free-ranging – even anonymous – society tends to express itself much less in this ritualistic way. Nevertheless, she has, we may hope, refuted that over-simplification which was so rife in the fifties of this century and which persisted in speaking of man as outgrowing his environment in a historical straight line so that the more primitive expressions of ritual and cult were attributed to

147

primitive man, with the inference that modern man came of age in an automatically secular environment and, furthermore, that the only voice in the name of Christianity which could appeal to such a secular age was a voice which was pitched within the same secular range.

So, perhaps rather more abrasively, Andrew Greeley, the American sociologist, bluntly states: 'The basic human religious needs and the basic religious functions have not changed very notably since the late ice age; what changes have occurred make religious questions more critical rather than less critical in the contemporary world'.[2] Certainly the pastoral experience of the author of this book, who has been largely located in London as a priest and bishop over twenty years, would not suggest to me that we live in a society which could be written off as secular as such. While it is true, on the lines which Mary Douglas argues, that there are many elements in a large western metropolis which break up recognizable communities of earlier times and which therefore encourage the fragmentation of those communities in the name of anonymity, it is not true to say that contemporary urban man is *a priori* secular.

A far more perceptive analysis was in fact offered in the inaugural lecture given by C. S. Lewis when he took his newly founded chair in English at Cambridge as long ago as 1954. 'It is hard to have patience', wrote Lewis, 'with those Jeremiahs, in press or pulpit, who warn us that we are "relapsing into paganism". It might be rather fun if we were. It would be pleasant to see some future Prime Minister trying to kill a large and lively milk-white bull in Westminster Hall. But we shan't. What lurks behind such idle prophecies, if they are anything but careless language, is the false idea that the historical process allows mere reversals; that Europe can come out of Christianity, "by the same door as in she went" and find herself back where she was. That is not what happens. A post-Christian man is not a pagan: you might as well think that a married women recovers her virginity by divorce. The post-Christian is cut off from the Christian past and therefore doubly from the pagan past.'[3] There it would seem is a far more perceptive analysis – at least in western society than the rather bland assumptions about a secular age. The truth is that in large urban communities there are ingredients which make it more difficult to relate to people and for people to relate to one another in corporate and cultic forms which in earlier ages were far more recognizable. Furthermore – and in addition to this – we have the reality (again predominant in the west) of a post-Christian society which is left with the hangovers of Christian faith, half truths and untried assumptions about Christianity, half empty churches which are not the same as half full ones!

In fact, as we can see in the opening chapters, starved of religion and the cult, contemporary man has gone out to find the very food of which he has been starved but now in synthetic and easily packaged forms. Archbishop John Habgood, in his book, *Church and Nation in a Secular Age* reaffirms the substantial place of cults in our contemporary world which have filled the vacuum left by the more orthodox faith of the Churches. His thesis is to question the assumption that our age is secular, though sadly he appears to do this with a view to reasserting a continuing role for the established Church – the status quo of a national Church – at the heart of English society. Yet there can be little doubt that if Christianity is to address itself to the society of today, it must discover the place of folk religion, the cult and the social and community ritualistic experiences of that religion as a starting point for its mission and its evangelism. Alan Wilkinson, in his book *The Church of England and the First World War*, rightly draws our attention to the Church's failure to grasp the significance of 'inarticulate religion outside the Church'.[4] Instead we have sought in a presupposedly secular society to market an antiseptic and largely cerebral religion – even at times a rather moralistic religion, purified from the 'primitive' ingredients of ritual and the supernatural yet hopelessly impotent to reach down into the subsoils of religious awareness which are still there in twentieth century man. For such a Church will be powerless to create and strengthen communities of faith in large cities where anonymity and fragmentation are rife. So much of the pastoral strategy and reforms of the fifties and sixties were the wrong treatment for a largely wrong diagnosis of the condition of contemporary society. The solution, as we shall hopefully see, is something much more radical and much more demanding, not least for a heavily institutionalized Church like the Church of England in particular, or even like Anglicanism in general.

For, if Lewis is right in his diagnosis of a predominantly post-Christian era, then there is a great deal of homework and teaching, pre-evangelism and sturdy apologetics to be undertaken if we are to redress wrong attitudes and half digested understandings of Christian faith. The ingredient within the tripartite model of Anglicanism of reason and human understanding will certainly be called upon heavily in the present climate to meet such a challenge. For a half empty bottle and a half full one will look alike, but they are very different in practice. In a straightforward missionary situation on virgin territory even a small number of committed Christians grow in numbers and 'fill up' in a straightforward way. But in our western world the existing Christians may in many ways (until they are converted) be an actual hindrance to further mission and evangelism. Karl Rahner writes, 'To adopt the language of Augustine, there will be many who may "at heart" belong to the Church in a way that is more efficacious for salvation than that of some Christians who belong to the "body" who are in the Church merely in a religio-sociological sense'.[5] The enemies of faith are within as well as without. Furthermore, the evangelistic thrust of the Church of England in particular (perhaps rather more than Anglicanism in general) finds itself addressing itself to just those parts of society which give the appearance of offering potentially strong opportunities for a presentation of the gospel but in reality prove no longer to be the effective channels and chains of Christian communication that they were in former ages. For example, a bishop in the Church of England is daily torn between servicing faithfully and responding positively to the invitations which come to him through the establishment (for the want of a better word), while he is very much aware that the more informal and ad hoc and seemingly fragile links and opportunities which are put before him are nevertheless almost certainly very real and far more authentic, as well as more likely to bear fruit in new life and Christian conversions.

2. The challenge to the Church of England

All this is much more difficult and presents a more radical challenge to Anglican Christians in the mother Church of England than it appears to do in the other world-wide provinces of the Anglican Communion. As I hinted in a previous chapter, there is no point, it seems to me, in going for the disestablishment of the Church of England for its own sake. Such a move *per se* would not necessarily achieve the ends which are so important for any revitalization of Anglicanism. You cannot and certainly should not seek to cut yourself off from the roots of history. It needs something perhaps of the spirit of the maverick to take the best of the past and yet to be free enough from that past to be flexible enough to respond to the present and so to be in a position to form the future.

There are, in fact, geographical areas in the British Isles where many of the old patterns of pastoral care, parochial worship and evangelism still work effectively. Where this is so, they should be allowed to continue. Yet alongside these, even at times strangely interwoven with these more traditional patterns, there really is a strong need to break loose and to encourage an alternative Church – a more gathered Church alongside the parochial and community Churches of the past. In places where there is a strong sense of community and where the parochial system still works it is surely still possible to build upon that sense of community with more traditional patterns of worship and corporate Christian life. In a rather simplistic way we tend to think of these as predominantly in the more rural areas. This is in fact a vast over-simplification. There are places in the inner city which are still almost villages and which still have an almost cultic view of their corporate life with a strong sense of the local community. Equally there are whole villages today which are restless with homelessness and fragmented by the commuter life-style. Both town and country alike will probably need, to varying degrees, the pastoral strategy of *both* the community Church and also the gathered Church: the traditional framework of services at set and traditional times in the traditional setting of the church building with all that tends to go with that, but at the same time and alongside it, alternative patterns of the gathered Church, at all sorts of times and in all sorts of places, catering for and even helping to form a life-style which would be almost totally foreign to the more traditional understanding of the community and parochial Church.

But is the Church of England sufficiently flexible for this kind of pluralism? Are its resources and places, clergy and church buildings, sufficiently mobile to respond to fragmentation and reorientation. It is often interesting to observe the Roman Catholic Church at work in England – in a country where it is a missionary body even still, and where it is not so tied into the establishment, placing a strong emphasis on the gathered Church, with neither more nor less buildings than they need, more or less located in the right places, they display just that very flexibility which the heavily institutionalized Church of England necessarily seems to lack through its historical roots in the past. To some extent this is inevitable and, of course, in other parts of the world, the situation is the very reverse and in fact it is Anglicans who enjoy in those places similar flexibility and the apparent advantage of seeming to travel light. We must certainly not make the mistake of supposing that the Church of England is typical of Anglicanism on a world-wide scale. It certainly is not. Indeed there would be many who would perhaps share the impatience of the author of this book at the untypical attitude and outlook of the Church of England when it is viewed alongside the other provinces of the world-wide Anglican Communion.

Nevertheless, the challenge to the Church of England in a post-Christian age, in which there are strong strands of secularization at work is formidable. It is easy to talk about a pluralistic approach – the desire to have the best of both worlds: the community Church and the gathered Church.

Sometimes it feels in practice as though this is really not possible. The danger in fact is so often that we shall end up with the very opposite of the best of both worlds – namely, falling between two stools: losing the friends we have had and yet failing to convince our enemies whom we have not yet won. Over many recent national issues for example, such as the nuclear debate or the question of the Falklands Thanksgiving Service, the Church of England, far from being either the Tory party at prayer on the one hand or even the via media on the other hand, came under sharp attack from those who traditionally have certainly claimed some allegiance to the established Church. At the same time the Church of England is not particularly conspicuous in its ability to convince (or certainly to convert) those who have traditionally been thin in numbers in the ranks of Anglicanism or even in Christianity at all in English society.

Yet alongside many continuing traditional practices of Anglicanism, there simply must be some radical ingredients of change if Anglicanism, humanly speaking, is to survive into the next century. Some writers, such as Karl Rahner, would put this point more strongly and make a passionate plea for a Church and a Christianity of the counterculture. 'The situation of Christians and thus of the church today is therefore one of transition from a peoples' church, corresponding to the former homogeneous, secular society and culture, to a church of that community of believers who entirely dissociate themselves, in virtue of a personal free decision in every case, from the current opinions and the feelings of their social environment, and who also find and imprint on properly theological faith its special character, perhaps precisely in and through a critical attitude to their society and its ruling forces.'[6] Can Anglicanism, heavy with the history of institutional Christianity respond to this kind of challenge? While facing the inevitable reality that the old-style Church will and must continue, has Anglicanism got within itself the resources for this kind of ferment? It is the deep conviction of this author that it has most certainly within its very mandate precisely the flexibility, checks and balances, which make possible the inevitable tensions and strain – if we are to be faithful to the mandate which this book has been at such pains to explore. For, rightly handled, those tensions and strains will themselves be productive of just the kind of flexibility that is required in holding together both the more institutionalized pastoral strategy of the past and these more ad hoc and community-based cells of Christian life in the future.

However, before we are ready fully to answer that challenge we need to see in a little more detail the shape of things to come and something of the ingredients that will predominate in the kind of ferment of which we have been speaking.

3. The Church of the 'little flock'

For the hard reality which faces Christians in all parts of the world in which Christianity has been formative in previous ages, is that churchgoing is going and it has almost gone! That is to say that, however well the formal institution of the church in a community runs its life, from its choir and music to its preaching and presentation, its pastoral care and missionary endeavour, there is not going to be on any appreciable scale a large number of what we used to call the 'friendly fringe'. They were those folk who were supposed to wake up perhaps on Easter Sunday morning, and decide that it would be quite a nice thing for them to go to church on this particular morning! The successful church had its doors conspicuously open to the friendly fringe and if things were going well the friendly fringe moved slowly into the more committed centre of church life. There would always perhaps be some portion of people who, in this rather haphazard and unpredictable way, related to a living church. But in the future the living heart of the Church will be made up of men and women who have come to a living faith and who seek to express that faith not so much by 'church-going habits' but much more by being the Church seven days a week both individually and corporately. Their whole lifestyle will be as gathered Christians, often living in some sort of cell or community, meeting for prayer, Eucharist and study and seeking to serve the wider community in a conspicuously Christian way. Such cells of life, community or alternative churches, will often have a strong sense of all-member ministry and may sit rather lightly to the established, ordained and clearly authorized forms of ministry as we have known them in the more mainstream Churches over the centuries. But the noteworthy factor about such new life in all the Churches will be that such Christians will have been 'won' from the post-Christian or secular world in which they find themselves. These cell churches will be the salt of the whole institutional Church. Karl Rahner goes even further when he writes: 'It means more to win one new Christian from what we may call neopaganism, than to keep ten "old Christians"'.[7] He continues by asserting: 'The possibility therefore of winning new Christians from a milieu that has become un-Christian is the sole living and convincing evidence that even today Christianity has a real chance for the future'.[8]

Such a Church of the little flock will be necessarily essential if Christianity is truly to withstand those kind of forces which, according to Mary Douglas, quoted earlier, tend to make for secularization. Such cells of new life will create community life in the face of anonymity, and where there are no natural communities they will also train and equip men and women with 'a reason for the faith' that is in them. The choice for leaders of such a Church of the future, whether priests or bishops, will be especially important. In choosing such leaders, we shall need to ask, according to Karl Rahner, not so much whether 'he has adapted himself very smoothly to the traditional machinery of the Church, or whether he has done well what people expected of him in the light of the traditional behaviour patterns of office-holders in the church', but rather, 'if he has ever succeeded in getting a hearing from the "neopagans" and made at least one or two of these into Christians . . . even though he has hitherto acted perhaps very unconventionally, and – for some merely traditional Christians – "scandalously"'.[9] Such comments should perhaps be printed and framed on display not only in England when the vacancy-in-see commission meet and over the desks of the Archbishops' and Prime Ministers' appointments secretaries, but also in those seemingly more democratic methods of appointment both for parish priests and bishops in other parts of the Anglican Communion!

Of course there will be some who see the Church of the little flock as necessarily breeding the ghetto mentality. Yet surely this does not necessarily follow. The conventional Churches of our contemporary society are just as open to the dangers of the ghetto mentality – for such a mentality has nothing whatever to do with numbers. You can have a ghetto mentality with a large congregation of several hundred people, because it is all in the end a question of outlook and conviction and has little to do with size. In the New Testament, the three analogies used by Jesus for the relation of the committed to the world at large is that of light, leaven and salt. All three of these analogies point away from themselves and are certainly not ends in themselves. Good lighting does not draw attention to itself; leaven is lost in the lump and salt is used for the sake of the meat which it flavours or preserves and is certainly not seen as something to be relished for its own sake. The Church of the future can even less afford to have a ghetto mentality than the traditional church patterns of previous history. On the contrary it must be a Church in the future which is so priestly that it could never possibly be churchy. By priestly I mean representative of the community in which it is set and representing that society in intercession, prayer and service before God. By definition a Church which sees itself as having a priestly character as the very mark of its distinctiveness, could never possibly react into a ghetto mentality. On the contrary, it is *the* distinction which exists in the New Testament between life in the kingdom and life outside. For all life in the kingdom will essentially be life for others: life outside (or before the kingdom) is always predictably every man for himself. That is the essence of a ghetto mentality and has nothing whatever to do with the size of a congregation, church or cell, and neither is it limited to ecclesiastical institutionalism.

4. Not so much an organization, more a way of life!

The movement from unfaith to faith will increasingly be

evident and at all times a dramatic pilgrimage in the Church of the future. It is not insignificant that at most Confirmation Services today, the bishop is vividly aware of a new kind of candidate who is increasingly conspicuous among the ranks of the confirmed. The numbers of young men and women coming to faith in later years and frequently to Confirmation (and Baptism) have substantially increased. Such commitment requires and demands that mere church-going will certainly not be enough. There is a real need for such new Christians to be sustained by many ingredients which have sadly only been partly available in the Churches of a more traditional pattern over recent centuries and at the present time. They will need to study and know their faith, not only in an intellectual and cerebral way but at many different levels. Sheer pressure of other disciplines and sciences which raise so many questions in the contemporary world cannot be countered only by 'a simple faith' or by certain spiritual experiences. The truth of the gospel is and must remain the main plank in the platform of Christian apologetics. Is Christianity true and, if it is, how can it be demonstrated that it is true? There is no escaping from the challenge of all that the Renaissance in its many and various forms put to the Church. Nor should there be, if men and women are to come to a living and lively faith and to grow in that faith all the days of their life.

But other ingredients will be necessary and evident in Christian formation in the Church of the future. All the Churches must recognize 'the charismatic element which can never be completely regulated'[10], and that this is just as necessary as the ministry of holy orders in the renewed Church of today and tomorrow. For 'office is never simply identical with the Spirit, and can never replace him'. For 'office . . . is really effectively credible in the sight of men only when the presence of the Spirit is evident and not merely when formal mission and authority are invoked, however legitimate these may be'. The sacramental life of this cellular Church will need the charismatic: and the charismatic will most certainly need the sacramental. All this will demand necessarily a much less clericalized Church – a Church which is not afraid of member ministry, but which rather sees the need for the ordained ministry as most pertinent precisely because there is so much diverse ministry about the place that it needs ordering in the best sense of that word, in order to maintain the unity of the Spirit in a Church of vast diversity and healthy variety.

Furthermore, it will nave to be a Church, community or cell of deep spirituality – most evidently necessary among the laity who are daily standing at the crossroads of the conflict between the Church and the world. This will demand not only imaginative preaching and teaching from those who are responsible for these ministries, but it will demand the life of community (in some sense) and of contemplative prayer. For contemplative prayer is sacramentalism taken to its obvious conclusion and it always leads men and women out of the sanctuary to see the whole universe in the end as sacramental. Such a way of life will also demand a readily accessible ministry of healing and reconciliation, all rooted in a knowledge and love of scripture.

Inevitably, therefore, the Church of the future will be a Church from the roots. 'The Church of the future', Rahner confidently asserts, 'will be one built from below by basic communities as a result of free initiative and association.'[11] If this is so and if such churches, cells and communities are to be properly pastored and sustained with word and sacrament this will in its turn demand even more from the bishop and his priests. Are the clergy and especially the bishops ready for this demand upon their distinctive ministries? Only an episcopate stripped of prelacy and a priesthood stripped of clericalism can really set the laity free from churchiness and help them to be the priestly people of God for the sake of the whole world. There is not space in this book to develop this crucially important theme. Enough to say that there can be no lasting renewal of an episcopal Church without a radical renewal of the episcopate. To some extent it is inevitably a question of numbers. For the kind of authentic episcopal ministry envisaged in such a future Church, no one man can relate to several hundred parishes or several hundred clergy. His lifestyle and the demands made upon him will demand that he is much more closely associated with the local churches and that he relates very closely with his clergy in servicing the cells and communities of Christians for which he has oversight. Episcopacy will necessarily be a far less bureaucratic office in the Church of the future and a far more pastoral and prophetic office. It follows that bishops will only survive in that work if dioceses are smaller, both geographically and numerically.

And all this will inevitably lead to a Church which is demanding in its whole lifestyle and in its ethical characteristics. That is not the same as some new moralizing! Pastoral and ascetical theology must always remain the larger concern in which the Church is rightly committed to moral and ethical issues. Increased leisure and job-sharing will all accentuate a drive in two opposite directions: more and more fragmentation, isolation and anonymity on the one hand, or a return to much more (almost village-like) communities on the other hand. In the end it is only from within a community where we know and are known, love and are loved, that we can seek out God's best for us and respond to it. That is a million light years away from the new moralizing which has swept across many Protestant revivalist communities in recent years.

5. Where on earth does Anglicanism stand in all of this?

If, as this last chapter supposes, there is really to be a major shift in the relationship between the committed flock of Christ and their relationship to a post-Christian or secular orientated society, then we must ask ourselves whether or not Anglicanism can not only maintain a foothold in that society but move from a mere position of maintenance to a position in which it is poised for mission. Can it be the kind of Church of which Karl Rahner speaks, which has the potential to win new Christians from what he calls neopaganism, or will it be heavily weighted in the direction of maintaining the old style Christianity for old style Christians? There will always be a role of some sort, at least in the foreseeable future for the latter, but if it were the sole *raison d'être* for Anglicanism, it would reduce Anglicanism from any vision of being in any real sense part of the world-wide fellowship of Catholicism.

It must be said that at the present moment this question is evenly poised in the balance and that it is hard frankly to see which way the debate will move. If, after all, the Anglican witness was nothing more than a particular religious and social tailoring of Catholicism, made to fit the social, economic, political, spiritual and intellectual needs of western Europe at a particular point in its development, then time will prove that there is not in fact within Anglicanism the resources of a Catholicism which will permit the kind of change, development and flexibility essential for any worldwide Catholic faith in a rapidly changing society. For that is the essence of Catholicism: this incredible ability to be pruned and even transplanted yet nevertheless to burgeon with new life in varying environments and different climates. These are hard words, but they have to be said. However well-tailored Methodism was in eighteenth, nineteenth and twentieth century English society, it has simply not proved to be sufficiently Catholic in its flexibility and resources to meet a totally changing sociological and economic situation in the United Kingdom today. That is not to criticize or demean the particular witness of Methodism. On the contrary it is a judgement upon Anglicanism, that such a renewal movement in the eighteenth century was ignored and marginalized by Anglicans who were too rigid and introverted to see a movement of the Spirit when it was under their very noses.

Yet the time is now ripe to put the same question to Anglicanism. Time alone will tell by the very end of this century whether or not the Anglican Church was just another experiment in fashion-tailoring, leaving the newly-trimmed organization and institution hoist with its own petard, or whether there really is sufficient fullness of Catholic life in Anglicanism to adapt, as only an organism can, to the worldwide needs of a radically changing society.

It is in fact the thesis of this book that Anglicanism has already showed such a potential for organic adaptation in the past and present and that it is in many ways uniquely poised for such a witness in the coming years. Its tripartite mandate — a Church of the Reformation and the Renaissance, but also a

Church of catholic order – should give to Anglicanism precisely that ability for response rather than reaction, which is so sorely needed at moments of change like our own. It must be freely admitted that eighteenth century Anglicanism would lead us to put a severe question mark over a prognosis which was too optimistic. There was no need for Methodism to have been expelled from Anglicanism. It was a time when the Church of England was not exercising its full three part model and when in the name of latitudinarianism there was a tendency to place reason and human insight above tradition and the Bible.

There are similar challenges to Anglicanism in the last decade of the twentieth century which will test the Anglican ethos today and tomorrow as Methodism tested it in the eighteenth century. Hopefully, this time it will not be found wanting. The first of these arises from within the Churches and the second arises from outside – from the witness of the world itself and the society in which the Church is placed.

The first of these challenges focuses on the shape of ministry and the place of the charismatic renewal. There can be no doubt that the charismatic renewal movements in the Churches have rubbed off on us all and that we are different because of it. *Laus Deo*. There was and there is a rigidity both in evangelical witness and in Catholic Church order which, left to themselves, without the Spirit, degenerate into formalism and dryness. Church order needs Holy Spirit. But equally it has to be said that there is a dangerous subjectivity, frothiness and, strangely (by inversion), a kind of formalism in a charismatic-centred Church without the checks and balances of the sacramental life and its attendant objectivity and without Church order and a regularized ordained ministry. The charismatic needs the Catholic sense of the sacraments and Church order. Furthermore, in a healthy Church there is a continuing tension which is only held in unity by a lively and authentic episcopal oversight. Indeed that is precisely the place of episcopacy, to oversee a living Church bursting with a diversity of charismatic ministries. For at the moment Anglicanism is crying out for evangelists, healers and above all perhaps for the ministry of discernment. None of these are necessarily located in, or coterminous with, the threefold orders of the ordained ministry as we now know them. There is no reason why they should be, though it would seem wholly appropriate that healing should be closely related to the ministry of reconciliation and also that discernment might be distinctively coveted by the bishops and their representatives – the priests of the Church.

Nevertheless, the ministry of the baptized is here to stay. Baptism is ordination to that sort of life within the priestly community which is perhaps best specified as life laid down – life for others. Such is the chemistry of the priesthood of all believers, the whole people of God. In that body, the deacon stands supremely as the sign to all believers of their distinctive status and so rescues them from an understanding of priesthood which would all too easily degenerate into sacerdotalism and ecclesiasticism. It is to be hoped that the Church of England will sooner rather than later wake up to the place of the perpetual diaconate which has been for a long time a feature within the rest of Anglican and Catholic world-wide Christianity.

The bishop, with his hands and arms – his priests – will exercise a ministry of word and sacrament in relation to the whole body of Christ with caring oversight and with a pastoral ministry which will build up the body in every way. So the whole body will be sustained for its ministry not only within the Church but within society. Yet in all this the renewal of charismatic witness and ministry presents a new challenge to Catholic order – a challenge which it should be well placed for in a healthy Anglicanism where there are the checks and balances of evangelical witness and experience, Catholic Church order and a place for reason and the witness of the created order. Time will tell whether we can really respond to this breath of renewal, which will radically reshape ministry and give to it, hopefully, the kind of flexibility which it will require to service the changing patterns and forms of Christian corporate life in a fragmenting society. For it is from that fragmenting society that the second challenge comes. Faster, cheaper international travel and all the technology of word processing and telecommunication will shrink the world and make us all the inhabitants of a global village, where Christianity can no longer claim the privileges and opportunities of the past for its mission and its evangelism. The parochial system as it is exercised rather specifically in the Church of England, or its adaptation throughout the rest of the Anglican provinces will not in itself sustain Christian life in the twenty-first century. We have indicated alternative structures of cells and communities which are already with us. 'Is it not the most urgent task of those, whoever they may be, who direct the destiny of the Christian community, to maintain the level of this vital conflict and to guarantee for all a flow of life between the institutional and the non-institutional? For today the Church is on both sides. To recognize and to live this fact is a primary duty.'[12] It is a Church which has the kind of tripartite model which we have been at pains to explain throughout this book which should be uniquely poised for this kind of challenge. What is clear is that although folk religion makes a sacramental and cultic ministry still possible even in the inner city, such an exclusive ministry is not made of sufficiently tough fibre to clothe the faithful with the necessarily intellectual and moral armour so necessary for Christians living in the world of the twentieth and twenty-first century. We must build our pastoral strategy on whatever is the given in the secular community. Christianity must, of course, be incarnational and rooted in the soil of the world in which it comes to birth. So there is rightly a place for the sacramental and this is increasingly being realized not only by Anglicans but by the Free Churches and Christians of all persuasions. For without it there is no real contact with the world which we are seeking to serve and which Christ longs to save.

Yet at the same time it must be admitted that a sacramentally centred Christianity without the challenge of reason and a strong diet of scriptural spirituality will simply not be sufficiently robust to withstand the challenges of a contemporary and largely secular society. In a survey in 1983 by MARC Europe it was shown that Roman Catholic churches, while having the largest *average* attendance in England, were losing the highest numbers of attenders each year. The cult of sacramental worship, unfed by the word and unchallenged by human reason will only continue in a stable society in which the structures and forms permit a strongly corporate sense of identity and at the same time underpin the very teachings of the Church and a Christian view of human relationships. The fragmentation and anonymity of much secularization demands that the Church forms its own cells and related communities and that these in their turn are formed around not only sacramental ministry but also around a teaching and preaching of the word of God in scripture which is open at all times to the dialectic of reason in its dialogue with the human spirit.

For it is not true to say that the working class of the people of the inner city will not undertake this and sit down and discuss their faith. It will not be scheduled of course at times and in ways which the more middle-class, university trained clergy would perhaps have liked. Yet in continuity with those strong working class movements such as trade unionism and the Labour movement, given the environment for discussion, debate and argument, it has always been part of the agenda of every class in society at all times and in all places to undertake this kind of corporate discussion and exploration of truth and faith. Furthermore, such exploration cannot be suppressed for long and its total suppression will soon lead to sectarian mentality, new divisions in the Church and a falling away of church membership.

In some sense, therefore, this book can end on an optimistic note as far as the future of Anglicanism is concerned. Whether or not Anglicanism survives and expands as a separate Church within the fellowship of world-wide Catholicism is almost an academic and irrelevant point. Hopefully, if renewal in all the Christian Churches continues, the distinctive witness of that tripartite model of Anglicanism will be lost in the plenitude or fullness of Christ's One Holy Catholic Church, and Anglicanism will cease to exist as a distinctive witness within Catholicism. Whether on the other hand the point of convergence of all the Churches in that plenitude of which we spoke earlier is within history or is eschatological is equally unforeseeable and equally irrelevant. The important challenge is a renewed faithfulness to a fullness already latent within Anglicanism itself which at its best should act as a kind of leaven within all the Christian Churches and therefore would presumably be lost in the end in any distinctive or separate sense. It is hard to see which way this will go and in some sense there is not much future in trying to determine the outcome of this process at this point. For unity within Anglicanism is always at best rather tenuous and at times even perilous. Yet within the twenty-seven provinces of the Anglican Church it would appear that there is a real understanding of an Anglican ethos along the lines which this book has suggested and that in the past and present this has given to Anglicanism a kind of flexible Catholicism which should stand it in good stead in the future.

6. The transfiguration of Christianity

Let us not be ashamed to admit, in conclusion, that a religious faith such as Christianity, with its roots necessarily deeply embedded in the economic, social and political soils of history, will be both formed and deformed by that history. It is the price we pay and the risk that God takes with a revelation which is incarnate. Yet Christianity at its best has always been suspicious of a purely spiritual view of the Church which seeks to keep it clinically antiseptic and uninvolved with the institutional forms and packaging of the age and environment in which it seeks to witness and minister. Anglicanism, perhaps neither significantly more nor less than any other of the Christian Churches, has a history in which there have been chapters when it has conformed to its environment and become deeply conditioned by those surroundings in ways which have led to scandal and disillusionment. Instead of the Church seeking to transform the world, a times like these, it has found itself frequently becoming almost indistinguishable from the very surroundings in which it has been formed. At such times and under such conditions, to speak of the Church as a sacra-

165

ment of the gospel, appeared in the eyes of many to be little better than blasphemous.

Yet, in fairness, it must be said that often at such moments of conformity to the world's standards, reformation and renewal were seldom far round the next turning in the road. Individual Christians formed groups and cells of protest which recalled the whole Church to a truer form of itself. Nevertheless, at their best, these movements of renewal did not encourage Christians to turn their backs on the world, nor to set themselves up above the decay and decadence of that world. After all, the Church is in the world in order that it may continue Christ's redeeming activity for the sake of the world. It does this best, not be being totally out of touch with the world but rather by being the salt and leaven within that world. Furthermore, whenever Christians have responded to the call of the Holy Spirit to reform and renewal, this has repeatedly (and not surprisingly) led to opposition – frequently fierce – from the powers that be in society. It is not an accident that the words witness and martyrdom are derived from the same Greek word: full and true witness will always evoke opposition and persecution from the world. Indeed Christ cautioned his Church against the implications of popularity with the world and with society.

Yet the goal of renewal must never be to stimulate or encourage martyrdom or opposition for its own sake. Rather the goal of renewal is never to take us out of the world but rather to make the Church more and more truly a sacrament of the gospel within the world. That is to say that the Church should become more and more truly, in its outward and visible form, a sign of the inner life of Christ by which it is possessed. After all the Church is the body of Christ – that is to say, it should bear the features of Christ in its outward face and image in such a way that men and women are drawn to share in its inward and hidden life.

In the accounts of the Transfiguration in the New Testament, we are told that as Christ prayed on the holy mountain the appearance of his face was changed. In self-conscious moments, the Church generally (and not least

Anglicanism in particular) has been concerned about its image. In the fifties and sixties there was much talk of how the image of the Church could become more appealing to the world. But as so often we were starting from the wrong end. As the Church and as Christians enter more and more fully into the mystery of Christ within us, seeing that alone as the only true hope of glory, so our face will automatically be changed and transfigured. Men and women get the face they deserve by the time they are forty; for our face is an outward sign of our inner life. So with the image of the Church. But the reordering of outward forms can never move faster than the recovery of inward life, and it is the former which must follow from the latter and which must claim our undivided attention.

Yet also in the story of the Transfiguration we are told that such an event pointed forward to the 'exodus' which Jesus was to accomplish in Jerusalem. In other words, transfiguration both prepares and points to passion, suffering and death. In South America, in Africa and in those parts of the world where Christians are being persecuted for their faith, there is increasing evidence of transfiguration, for it was transfiguration and renewal which inevitably called forth that persecution and opposition in the first place. Yet if the Christian Churches are increasingly to become sacraments and signs of Christ's redeeming love and work, evermore truly conformed to his inner life, then they will inevitably share in his passion for the sake of the world.

In the white heat of that transforming renewal, unity will be inevitable and witness increasingly effective. It is in that context that the Churches will be purified, not, however, in order to become pure for themselves or for the sake of their own glory, but in order that such renewed life may be in its turn 'laid down' for the sake of the salvation of the world and in preparation for the handing over of the kingdom. In such a process, discussions about denominations and the merits of various theological methods and models will be irrelevant because they will have by then become redundant. The truth will be enfleshed and its authority will be self-evident. Yet discussions about various traditions and teachings in the history of

Christianity will only have become redundant because, in the first place, they pointed and prepared the way for precisely 'that hour'. When it will be or how it will come is not for us to say – for it has never been for us to know the 'times and seasons' which have always been in the knowledge of the Father.

To us belong the more humble and less obvious tasks of faithfulness to a tradition which has brought us to where we stand, yet which always points us beyond to further renewal and deeper conformity to the mind and will of Christ as we come to know them. If we set any discussions about our faith and practice as Christians in this fuller context, there need be no danger for a book like this or indeed for any debate along these lines degenerating into a reassertion of brash denominationalism. But rather it is precisely because we do not consider ourselves to have obtained all this nor yet to be perfected by it, that we press on and try 'to make it our own', 'straining forward to what lies ahead' and pressing on 'toward the goal for the prize of the upward call of God in Christ Jesus' (Phil. 3. 12–14).

NOTES

1. Mary Douglas, *Natural Symbols*, Penguin edition, 1970, p. 36
2. Andrew M. Greeley, *The Persistence of Religion*, SCM Press Ltd, 1973, p. 1
3. C. S. Lewis, *De descriptione temporum*, They asked for a paper, Geoffrey Bles, 1962, p. 20
4. Alan Wilkinson, *The Church of England and the First World War*, SPCK, 1978, p. 89
5. Karl Rahner, *The Shape of the Church to Come*, SPCK, 1974, p. 74
6. Ibid. p. 23
7. Ibid. p. 32
8. Ibid.
9. Ibid. p. 33
10. Ibid. p. 57
11. Ibid. p. 108
12. Paul Ricoeur, *Le Monde*, 19 July 1973

Acknowledgements

The Author wishes to express his thanks to the following for permission to reproduce material of which they are the authors, publishers or copyright holders.

The Rt Revd Gerald Ellison for an extract from *The Anglican Communion* (The Seabury Press, New York).

Routledge & Kegan Paul Ltd and Princeton University Press for extracts from *The Collected Works of C. G. Jung* trans. R. F. C. Hull, Bollingen Series XX, Vol. 10: *Civilization in Transition*. Copyright © 1964, 1970 by Princeton University Press.

Collins Publishers for extracts from *The Third Wave* by Alvin Toffler and *Teilhard de Chardin, Scientist and Seer* by C. E. Raven.

Penguin Books Ltd for extracts from *Bede: A History of the English Church and People*, trans. Leo Sherley-Price (Penguin Classics, Revised edition 1968) pp. 73, 86–87. Copyright © Leo Sherley-Price 1955, 1968.

Hutchinson Publishing Group Limited for an extract from *Natural Symbols* by Mary Douglas (Barrie & Rockliff).

Longman Group Ltd for extracts from *The Gospel and the Catholic Church* by A. M. Ramsey and *Gore to Temple* by A. M. Ramsey.

Hodder and Stoughton Limited for a poem by A. F. Balfour in *Nurslings of Immortality* by Raynor C. Johnson.

The Society for Promoting Christian Knowledge for extracts from 'What is Anglican Theology?' by A. M. Ramsey in *Theology Vol. XLVIII* (1945); *Doctrine in the Church of England: English Spirituality* by Martin Thornton; *The Lambeth Conferences (1867–1930)*; *The Lambeth Conference 1968*; and *The Shape of the Church to Come* by Karl Rahner.

SCM Press Ltd for an extract from *Essays in Liberality* by A. R. Vidler.

Oxford University Press for an extract from *Roman Britain and the English Settlements* by R. G. Collingwood and J. N. L. Myres.

Darton Longman & Todd Ltd, London, for an extract from

Canterbury and Rome–Sister Churches by Robert Hale (published and copyright 1982).

A. R. Mowbray & Co. Ltd for extracts from *Anglicanism* by Stephen Neill and *The Integrity of Anglicanism* by Stephen W. Sykes.

George Weidenfeld and Nicolson Ltd for extracts from *Anglicanism in History and Today* by J. W. C. Wand.

Lutterworth Press for two extracts from *Christianity and Science* by Charles E. Raven.

Morehouse-Barlow Co. Inc., Connecticut, for extracts from *Anglican Spirituality* edited by William Wolf and *The Future of the Church* by A. M. Ramsey.

Robin Mead, TNL Syndication Department for an extract from an article by Peter Baelz entitled 'Reconsidering Anglicanism's interdependent traditions' in *The Times* issue dated 27 November 1982, © Times Newspapers Ltd.

T & T Clark Limited for extracts from *The Spirit of Anglicanism* edited by William J. Wolf.

Van Nostrand Reinhold (UK) Co. Ltd for extracts from 'The Authority of the Bible' by A. M. Ramsey in *Peake's Commentary on the Bible*.

Adam and Charles Black Publishers for an extract from *The Spirit of Anglicanism* by H. R. McAdoo.

Geoffrey Chapman, a division of Cassell Ltd, for extracts from *Dialogue between Christians* by Yves Congar.

The Seabury Press, New York, for an extract from *Anglican Congress 1963*, E. R. Fairweather (Ed.), © 1963.

Humanities Press, Atlantic Highlands, NJ 07716, for an extract from *Anglicanism in Ecumenical Perspective* by W. H. Van de Pol.

A. P. Watt Ltd, Literary Agents, for an extract from *Only One Earth* by Barbara Ward.